Fringe Benefits and Overtime Behavior

Fringe Benefits and Overtime Behavior

Theoretical and Econometric Analysis

Ronald G. Ehrenberg
University of Massachusetts

Lexington Books
D. C. Heath and Company
Lexington, Massachusetts
Toronto   London

This report was prepared for the Manpower Administration, U.S. Department of Labor, under research grant number 91–15–69–40, authorized by Title I of the Manpower Development and Training Act. Since contractors performing research under Government sponsorship are encouraged to express their own judgment freely, the report does not necessarily represent the Department's official opinion or policy. Moreover, the contractor is solely responsible for the factual accuracy of all material developed in the report.

Portions of the material presented in Chapters 2, 3 and 7 have been previously published, and are reprinted with permission from *American Economic Review,* Vol. LX, No. 3 (June 1970), pp. 352–357; *Journal of Economic Theory,* Vol. III, No. 1 (March 1971), pp. 85–104; and *Western Economic Journal,* Vol. IX, No. 2 (June 1971), pp. 199–207.

Published simultaneously in Canada.

Printed in the United States of America.

International Standard Book Number: 0–669–75242–8

Library of Congress Catalog Card Number: 74–162640

Table of Contents

List of Tables

Acknowledgements

An earlier version of this study was submitted as a doctoral dissertation to the Department of Economics, Northwestern University. I am deeply indebted to Professors Frank Brechling, George Delehanty, Louis Maccini, Dale Mortensen, and Arthur Treadway for constructive comments during all stages of my research. Mr. Thomas Gavett and Mr. Samuel Cohen of the U.S. Bureau of Labor Statistics were instrumental in providing the data utilized in the study and I am extremely grateful to them for their assistance.

The bulk of the underlying research was generously supported by a grant from the Manpower Administration of the U.S. Department of Labor, while fellowships from the Woodrow Wilson Foundation and the National Defense Education Act supported the initial stages of the project. I am deeply indebted to these sponsoring organizations; however neither they nor any of the individuals cited above are responsible for the views expressed in this study or for any errors that remain.

In slightly different form, portions of the material presented in Chapters 2, 3 and 7 have been previously published in the *American Economic Review*, the *Journal of Economic Theory*, and the *Western Economic Journal*. Their permission to reprint the material is sincerely appreciated.

I am also grateful to Mrs. Jean Haefner for her expert typing of difficult material and especially to my wife Randy for her continual encouragement and support. Indeed her mere presence makes everything worthwhile.

This study was prepared under Grant No. 91–15–69–40 from the Manpower Administration, U.S. Department of Labor, under the authority of Title I of the Manpower Development and Training Act of 1962, as amended. Researchers undertaking such projects under government sponsorship are encouraged to express freely their professional judgment. Therefore, points of view or opinions stated in this document do not necessarily represent the official position or policy of the Department of Labor.

Finally this study is dedicated to my son Eric Lawrence and to the memory of Lawrence Birch.

Fringe Benefits and Overtime Behavior

1

Introduction

A rational manpower policy must seek to create jobs as well as to provide training for unemployed workers. The creation of new jobs has been hindered, however, by the observed tendency of employers to substitute overtime hours for additional employees, even while substantial unemployment exists. For example, in 1966, the year on which this study will focus, 55,376,000 hours of overtime were worked on average per week by production workers in the manufacturing industries at the same time that 3.2 percent of the manufacturing work force was unemployed.[1] If 25 percent of this overtime could have been eliminated and transformed into full-time jobs, production worker employment would have increased by over 2.4 percent. (This calculation is based on a production worker employment level of 14,199,000, see [71], p. A45, and assumes a forty-hour standard work-week for the new employees.)

Although a large proportion of overtime hours is due to disequilibrium phenomena such as rush orders, seasonal demand, mechanical failures, and absenteeism, there may exist a substantial amount of overtime which is regularly scheduled. A given level of labor services may be obtained by various combinations of hours per man and number of men, and there is no reason, a priori, that the optimal number of overtime hours per man should be zero in equilibrium. In particular, of crucial importance in influencing the optimal division of a firm's required labor input between a stock of employees and the average number of hours per week that each employee works, are those labor costs per employee that are independent of the exact number of hours of work. The higher these costs relative to the overtime wage rate, the more likely that overtime will be substituted for additional employment. These "quasi-fixed" costs include those labor turnover costs and supplementary compensation practices which are employee rather than man-hour related. The latter category contains most fringe-benefit costs of employers such as: paid vacations, sick leave, holidays, employer contributions to pensions, health insurance and other voluntary welfare and insurance plans, and some legally required payments.

To a large extent, the existence and economic effects of these fringe-benefit costs have been neglected by academic economists, although

---

[1] See *Premium Pay for Overtime under the Fair Labor Standards Act* [71], p. A45, and *Statistics on Manpower* [72], p. 17.

1

recognized by those in government.[2] Since 1959, the Bureau of Labor Statistics has been making periodic surveys of "supplementary compensation practices," while the Chamber of Commerce has conducted biennial studies of fringe benefits since 1947.[3] That the magnitude of these costs is not small can be seen by the Chamber of Commerce estimate that in 1965, fringe payments alone averaged 24.7 percent of total payroll costs for the firms in this sample.[4] Moreover, this percentage has been increasing over the postwar period. The growing importance of these costs was indeed a primary factor behind the formulation of the proposed congressional *Overtime Pay Penalty Act of 1964* [70]. This bill proposed that the Secretary of Labor be given discretionary power to increase the overtime premium in those industries where it was felt that "excessive" overtime was being used, with the hope of decreasing overtime and consequently increasing employment.

The primary purpose of this study is to construct models of the firm's short-run demand for workers and hours to be used as a framework in which to empirically ascertain the determinants of intraindustry cross-section variations in observed overtime hours per man. The study utilizes unpublished establishment data provided to us by the Bureau of Labor Statistics from their survey of "Employer Expenditures for Selected Compensation Practices, 1966." Of major interest are tests of the hypothesis stated above, that high fixed costs per man relative to the overtime wage rate induce a substitution of overtime hours for additional employment. On the basis of these tests, implications for manpower policy, such as the wisdom of increasing the overtime premium in any given industry or size class of establishments can be drawn.

The concentration in the empirical parts of the study on *intraindustry* variations in overtime hours per man is intentional and reflects our own methodological bias. The only previous study which attempted to empirically test the relationship between overtime and fringe benefits was a cross-section *interindustry* analysis by Van Atta [88] for 1959 and 1962, using mean values of the variables for each two-digit manufacturing industry as the units of observation.[5] Interindustry cross-section regressions require assumptions

---

[2] For an early exception see Joseph Garbarino [29]. Roger Waud [90] includes these costs in his study of total man-hour behavior in U.S. manufacturing but does *not* consider their implications for hours of work per man.

[3] For example, see B.L.S. Bulletin 1308 [78] and Chamber of Commerce of the United States, *Fringe Benefits* [13].

[4] See *Fringe Benefits 1965* [13], p. 9.

[5] Using aggregate annual time-series data, Van Atta also attempted to test this relationship for 1947–1965. As we observed earlier, the ratio of fringe benefits to the overtime wage rate had an almost steady upward trend during this period. Consequently, her estimated coefficients may be capturing the effects of any other variables with trends, that were omitted.

about the homogenity of production processes across industries which do not appear to be warranted. Moreover, there is a question as to whether industry means are appropriate units of observation. Table 1–1 presents for each two-digit manufacturing industry, the mean and within-industry standard deviation of observed annual overtime per man in 1966, calculated from the establishment data in our sample.[6] In most cases, the within-industry variation is substantial and consequently regressions using industry means as units of observation may obscure the underlying relationships further. It is not surprising, therefore, that Van Atta [88] did *not* find a statistically significant relationship in her work between overtime and the ratio of weekly fixed labor costs to the overtime wage rate. Disaggregation is necessary and undertaken in this study.

Table 1–1. Mean Values and Standard Deviations of 1966 Annual Overtime Hours Per Man for Manufacturing Establishments in the Sample

Industry	S.I.C. Code	Number of Observers	Mean Value Overtime	Standard Deviation Overtime
Ordinance	19	5	338.244	108.009
Food	20	86	164.511	165.090
Tobacco	21	5	94.293	111.812
Textile	22	143	187.598	127.401
Apparel	23	150	58.702	63.835
Lumber	24	31	169.596	156.258
Furniture	25	22	149.523	128.553
Paper	26	33	309.199	199.622
Printing	27	37	145.411	129.210
Chemicals	28	40	189.189	146.718
Petroleum	29	13	78.276	62.343
Rubber	30	24	221.510	142.938
Leather	31	19	74.258	56.390
Stone-clay-glass	32	110	214.014	141.541
Primary metal	33	77	220.541	122.468
Fabricated metal	34	92	206.807	151.789
Machinery	35	82	261.412	174.796
Electrical equipment	36	63	146.228	102.644
Transportation equipment	37	47	227.383	153.210
Instruments	38	16	215.169	131.441
Misc. manufacturing	39	24	139.768	140.552

Note: See the appendix to Chapter 4 for the method used in calculation of the individual establishment annual overtime/man variable.

---

[6] Similar data for the nonmanufacturing industries is found in Chapter 6. Description of the data and explicit calculation of the variables are found in Chapter 4 and its appendix.

The study is organized as follows: After briefly surveying previously related work, Chapter 2 presents several simple static and dynamic models of the firm's employment-hours decisions. The effect of both certainty and stochastic absentee rates on these decisions are discussed, as well as an econometric problem that may arise if all establishments in the survey are not in long-run equilibrium, as is usually assumed in cross-section econometric work. These models, as do previous models such as those of Brechling [9], Solow [67], and Nadiri and Rosen [51], are neoclassical in nature and ignore several important features of unionized labor markets. It is more appropriate, however, to incorporate such features directly into our theoretical models than to invoke their presence to explain anomalies in empirical results found when testing standard neoclassical models.

Consequently, in Chapter 3 we introduce such concepts as the heterogenity of labor, the internal labor market, the establishment wage structure and learning-by-doing into a model designed to explain the dynamics of the firm's employment-hours decisions. By incorporating these features, we are able to offer an explanation for why not all employees of a given establishment work the same amount of overtime and indicate the conditions under which it is rational for management to agree to union demands that overtime be assigned on the basis of seniority. We can also solve the problem discussed in Chapter 2 and indicate how cross-section regressions seeking to explain intraindustry variations in observed overtime hours will be affected by firms being in short-run equilibrium along the dynamic adjustment path, derived from the model, instead of all being in long-run stationary equilibrium. This is seen to be an aggregation problem, which is solvable within the assumptions of the model.

Chapter 4 provides a description of the data and discusses the problems involved in attempting to classify the various supplementary compensation items as "quasi-fixed" or variable, with respect to hours of work. The fact that observed overtime may not conform to the theoretically appropriate variable is discussed and several solutions proposed. The appendix to this chapter indicates explicitly how each of the variables used in the analysis was calculated.

Based on the models presented in Chapters 2 and 3, the next two chapters present empirical investigations of the determinants of intraindustry variations in observed overtime hours per man in U.S. manufacturing and non-manufacturing industries for 1966. Several interesting similarities and contrasts appear between the results for the two groups and these are noted. The final chapter provides a summary of the important results as well as the implications for manpower policy.

2 On the Short-Run Employment-Hours Decision

In this chapter, we present the underlying theoretical models that serve as a basis for both our empirical work and the theory developed in the following chapter. In contrast to much of the earlier literature on the determinants of hours of work, we view the level of overtime per man as being determined on the demand side by the employer, rather than on the supply side by the individual employees. Since others have recently adopted similar viewpoints, it is relevant to briefly cite and summarize previous related work and this is done in the first section of the chapter. The remaining sections consider several theoretical models of the short-run demand for workers and hours.[1] We initially present a static model similar to that found in Rosen [58]. This model is then extended to consider the effects of both certainty and stochastic absentee rates on the overtime-employment decision. The equilibrium solutions of these static models may be thought of as the stationary equilibrium solutions that are embedded in more general dynamic models. Consequently the final section outlines a dynamic model and indicates how hours of work vary along the equilibrium adjustment path derived from the model. Unless firms are all in stationary equilibrium, it is easy to observe that attempts to estimate the equilibrium relationship implied by the static models using establishment cross-section observations may yield meaningless regression coefficients. This result provides one of the motivations for the theory developed in the succeeding chapter.

A Brief Survey of the Literature

Much of the previous theoretical and empirical work seeking to explain time-series or cross-section variations in hours of work is based upon the neo-classical theory of household consumption–leisure decisions.[2] The implicit assumption upon which the empirical studies are based is that there is an

---

[1] The term ''short run'' is meant to connote a time period in which the firm takes its capital stock and output decisions as being predetermined and does not refer to the problem of adjustment to equilibrium levels at this point.

[2] Empirical contributions to this literature include Douglas [20], Finegan [26], Kosters [40], Feldstein [24], and Dymond and Saunders [21]. Recent theoretical contributions include Moses [48], Perlman [54], [55], and Brofenbrenner and Mossin [11] among others.

infinitely elastic *demand* for hours of work per employee; employers quote a wage rate and employees are free to choose the number of hours that they wish to work.

The approach taken in this study contrasts with the above. Rather than approaching variations in hours of work from the supply side, we approach it from the demand side. We consider models in which the various wage parameters are taken as given by the firm in the short run, either through collective bargaining or some other means. The firm then chooses an optimal mix of number of employees and overtime hours per man to minimize the costs of achieving a required level of labor services. That is, the firm is assumed to face infinitely elastic *supplies* of both men and hours per man at the prevailing wage parameters. We are arguing therefore, that there are always employees available who would be willing to work overtime at the existing overtime wage rate.[3] Given the asymmetry of market power between the firm and the *individual* employee, we believe that it is more plausible to assume that the firm is in equilibrium than to assume that all individuals are in equilibrium.

Several earlier studies have approached the determination of hours of work from the demand side. Brechling [9] and Ball and St. Cyr [4] present models of the employment-hours decisions, however, they neglect the quasi-fixed labor costs. The empirical sections of these papers concentrate on estimating "employment functions" rather than hours equations.[4]

Rosen [58], [59], Nadiri and Rosen [51], and Black and Kelejian [8] all present models of the employment-hours decision that include a fixed cost of labor. The first three interpret these costs in terms of specific-investment costs and replacement costs of quits, and ignore the effect of the quasi-fixed supplementary compensation costs on overtime. Since no data on specific investment costs are available, proxy variables are used in each of the studies. In his study of interoccupational differences in hours of work on Class-I railroads, Rosen [58] assumes that these costs are correlated with skill levels. Similarly, his study [59] of interindustry differences in average hours of work based on the 1/1,000 sample of the 1960 census of population uses worker attributes such as age, education level, marital status, and race as proxies

---

[3] That is, some labor is "underemployed" in the sense of Perlman [54].

[4] Other recent contributions to the employment-function literature include Brechling and O'Brien [10], Coen and Hickman [17], Fair [22], Hamermesh [31], Ketchum [39], Kuh [42], Nadiri [50], Smyth and Ireland [65], and Waud [90]. An excellent description and critique of the pre-1968 studies is found in Fair [22], ch. 2. All of the above take output as given; an alternative more general approach is to assume that the flow of new orders is given to the firm and that the firm makes inventory as well as employment decisions. This type of approach is pursued in Mortensen [47].

for labor quality and turnover rates, and correspondingly, specific investment costs. Nadiri and Rosen [51], in explaining aggregate time-series variations in hours of work, fail to find an adequate proxy variable for the fixed costs and hence omit them from the empirical work. As opposed to the first three papers, Black and Kelejian [8] explicitly recognize the effect of the various fringe-benefit costs on the overtime decision. As part of a five-equation model of the labor market, they estimate an hours equation using postwar aggregate quarterly data. However, since the ratio of fringe-benefit costs to the overtime wage rate has been increasing at a steady trend during the period, they include a time-trend rather than the fixed-cost variable in their empirical analysis. Consequently, it is impossible to separate the effect of the fixed costs on over-time from any omitted variable that also moves in a trend.

Mention should also be made of the studies by Kuh [41] and Fair [22] which attempt to explain time-series variations in hours paid for, at different levels of aggregation. These studies are demand oriented in that the employer is assumed to adjust hours in order to reach some equilibrium value (although the supply side is introduced via an unemployment rate variable which represents tightness in the labor market). However, both studies assume, at least implicitly, that the equilibrium value of hours involves zero overtime and ignore the importance of the fixed costs. That is, they view overtime as solely a transient response to a disequilibrium situation.

It should be realized that explanations of variations in hours of work that come from the supply and the demand sides of the market are not mutually exclusive. Indeed Rosen [59] has estimated a model that explains the simultaneous determination of wages and hours by forces of supply and demand. His study concentrates on *interindustry* differences using mean values from the 1/1,000 sample of the 1960 census of population, standardized for occupational composition. As he notes, however, "It is of course true that the observational units whose behavior is to be explained determine the most appropriate model design."[5] Within a single unionized industry, we are maintaining that the demand and supply model does not apply. More specifically, that there is some type of wage-setting process that yields wage parameters that then enter individual employers' demand for labor functions.[6] Rosen's [59] findings that the *interindustry* supply of labor is not infinitely elastic should not be thought of as contradicting our basic assumption that the

[5] Preliminary draft of [59] dated October 12, 1967, p. 2.

[6] A similar view is expressed by Lucas and Rapping [44]. Barzel [5] has written an interesting and yet unpublished paper dealing with the determination of hours and wages in a competitive labor market. We are reminded, however, of the remark attributed to Arnold Weber, "The invisible hand is all thumbs in the labor market."

supply of men and hours per man to an *individual establishment* is infinitely elastic.[7]

The next section presents the structure and assumptions of a simple static model, similar to that found in Rosen [58], which serves both to illustrate the firm's decision problem and to provide a basis for the following work.

A Simple Static Model of the Employment-Hours Decision

Given the level of output to be provided, the level of technology, and the flow of capital services, a neoclassical production function can be inverted to determine a unique required flow of labor services. The firm's decision problem is then to choose that combination of men and hours per man which will produce that flow, and which will minimize its labor costs. Symbolically, the problem is to

$$\text{minimize} \quad w_1 M + (r+q)TM + w_2 M\bar{H} + w_2 bM(H - \bar{H}) \quad \text{where } b > 1 \tag{2.1}$$

$$\text{subject to} \quad L = F(M, H) \tag{2.2}$$

where

$$\langle F_1, F_2 > 0 \rangle \tag{2.2a}$$

and

$$\langle (2F_1 F_2 F_{12} - F_1^2 F_{22} - F_2^2 F_{11}) - (2F_1 F_2^2 / M) > 0 \rangle \tag{2.2b}$$

Here w_1 represents those employment costs per man which are "fixed" in the sense of being independent of the exact number of hours that each employee works. These include the costs for such items as paid vacations, paid holidays, private welfare and insurance plans, and many legally required insurance payments. Some of these costs are annual, others monthly, still others weekly; the assumption here simply being that the employer imputes them to himself on a weekly basis. The next term represents what Rosen [58]

---

[7] Indeed using SMSA mean values as the units of observations, Cotterill [19] has found that cross-section intraindustry supply curves of men in the retail trade industries appear to be extremely elastic. His work uses a simultaneous supply and demand framework but ignores the hours decision.

and Nadiri and Rosen [51] have called the "user cost of labor." T represents the once-over turnover and investment cost per man of hiring and training workers. If these costs are financed by borrowing, they must be discounted by the interest rate (r) and also adjusted for replacement costs by the quit rate (q). Assuming that equilibrium occurs in the overtime region, the wage costs per man are the wage rate (w_2) times the maximum number of hours per man payable at straight-time wages $(\bar{H})$ plus the overtime wage rate $(w_2 b)$ times the number of overtime hours per man.

The constraint (2.2) asserts that the flow of labor services (L) is a function of the number of men employed (M) and the number of hours per man paid for (H). For a number of reasons discussed by Feldstein [23], it is inappropriate to specify the labor input as being equal to the number of man-hours paid for (MH).[8] Here we assume only that the marginal contribution to labor services of each input is positive over the relevant region and that the necessary condition (2.2b) for the optimizing problem to yield a minima is met. This condition requires that the marginal rate of substitution of men for hours be a decreasing function of hours, the usual convex isoquant assumption.[9]

Minimizing formula (2.1) subject to equation (2.2) yields the familiar marginal conditions that (where λ is a Lagrangian multiplier)

$$w_1 + (r + q)T + w_2 \bar{H} + w_2 b(H - \bar{H}) + \lambda F_1 = 0 \qquad (2.3a)$$

$$w_2 bM + \lambda F_2 = 0 \qquad (2.3b)$$

$$F(M, H) = L \qquad (2.3c)$$

Conditions (2.3a) and (2.3b) simply require that the ratio of the marginal contribution to labor services of an additional employee to that of an additional hour of overtime for all employees be equated to the ratio of the respective marginal costs of the two methods of increasing labor services. The above conditions can be solved for an equilibrium combination of men and hours per man (M^*, H^*) which are functions of all the parameters in the model. In particular

---

[8] These include the varying intensity of effort of labor due to fatigue and the varying ratio of hours worked to hours paid as the latter changes, due to the fixed costs in hours paid for (set-up time, coffee breaks, etc.). Rosen indicates that this idea can be traced back to Chapman [14].

[9] Actually, condition (2.2b) is stronger than the requirement of diminishing marginal rate of substitution between factors because a constant cost locus is not linear when viewed in (M, H) space. See [58], p. 515, for a graphical illustration of this point. Note that the labor input function $L = MH$ does *not* satisfy equation (2.26).

$$H^* = h(w_1, r, q, T, w_2, b, \overline{H}, L) \qquad h_1, h_2, h_3, h_4 > 0, \quad h_5, h_6, h_7 < 0 \quad (2.4a)$$

where

$$M^* = m(w_1, r, q, T, w_2, b, \overline{H}, L) \qquad m_1, m_2, m_3, m_4 < 0, \quad m_5, m_6, m_7 > 0 \tag{2.4b}$$

Explicit expressions for the values of these partials are presented in the appendix to this chapter but the interpretations of their signs is straightforward. An increase in the component of cost that is independent of hours $[w_0 = w_1 + (r + q)T]$ increases the marginal cost of labor through additional employment relative to the marginal cost of labor through added hours per worker. Consequently a substitution of overtime hours for employment occurs. Similarly an increase in the wage rate, the overtime premium, or the number of hours after which the overtime premium goes into effect, decreases the marginal cost of labor through additional employment relative to that through added hours per worker and induces a substitution of additional employment for overtime hours per man.

The effect of an increase in required labor services on equilibrium hours and employees depends upon the inferiority or noninferiority assumptions that we make about each input. Intuitively we feel that

$$\frac{\partial M^*}{\partial L} > 0, \qquad \frac{\partial H^*}{\partial L} = 0 \tag{2.4c}$$

That is, that equilibrium hours are invariant to scale. Given the cost parameters, a firm that faces a permanent increase in output may temporarily adjust overtime, but in the long run it will return to the previous equilibrium level of hours. The conditions under which this result will hold are found in the appendix to the chapter. In particular it is shown that the assumptions of: (1) homogenity of labor and (2) the marginal contribution to labor services of an hour of one employee being independent of hours of work of other employees are sufficient to guarantee this result. The invariance of hours to scale will be an important assumption in our empirical work since we possess no data on output or the metaphysical concept of labor services.

Absenteeism and the Overtime Decision[10]

The model presented above can be generalized to consider the effects of absenteeism. It is important to do this because upon reading the congressional hearings on the *Overtime Pay Penalty Act of 1964* [70], one cannot

---

[10] The results of this section have been presented in my paper "Absenteeism and the Overtime Decision," *American Economic Review*, June 1970. I am grateful to an anonymous referee of that journal for suggesting the diagrammatic approach taken in Figure 2–1 below.

11

fail to be impressed by the emphasis that management places on absenteeism as a primary cause of overtime. The argument given there is basically quite simple: Large firms, it is claimed, attempt to account for absenteeism by hiring stand-by workers; however, because of the stochastic nature of the absentee rate, it is impossible for them to have replacements always available. Hence, overtime must be worked by existing employees in order to meet production schedules. The conclusion one draws from this argument is that it is the randomness of absenteeism which is the cause of overtime and that if the absentee rate were known with certainty, then management could take account of it without recourse to additional overtime. Admittedly, this conclusion and the argument that follows neglect the indivisibilities inherent in small firms, union rules concerning the existence of stand-by workers, and the heterogeneity and scarcity of skilled labor—factors which tend to limit the employment of stand-by employees. Empirically, in industries in which these factors are prevalent, we would also expect that overtime be positively related to the absentee rate.

In this section we challenge the above conclusion and argue that a rational economic response to a certainty absentee rate involves *increasing* the amount of overtime worked per man, while the effect on the level of employment is ambiguous. Furthermore, we claim that a stochastic absentee rate leads to a larger optimal employment stock and, in at least one special case, an average to a *smaller* amount of overtime worked per man than in the certainty absentee rate case. Crucial to our argument is the observation that many of the labor costs which we classify as "fixed" must be paid by the employer even when an employee is absent, but overtime hourly wage payments need not be made to absentees.

Let us first introduce a certainty absentee rate into the model. Suppose that the firm knows that on any given day only the fraction a of its employees will be in attendance. Then its appropriate labor input function becomes

$$L = F(aM, H) \tag{2.5}$$

The inclusion of an absentee rate also modifies the cost function in a nonsymmetric way. In particular, the capitalized turnover costs must be paid regardless of whether an employee works on any given day (or week). Similarly many of the fixed employment costs such as health insurance, pension coverage, vacation pay, and unemployment compensation insurance are independent of the employee's attendance on any particular day.[11]

---

[11] This last statement should be qualified. Often no holiday pay is received unless the employee works the days directly before and after a paid holiday. Similarly unless a minimum number of days are worked, the employee is ineligible for vacation pay and pension credit. Also unemployment compensation insurance costs are man-hour (not man) related unless the employee's annual income is above a certain level. Finally, if the employee is "fired for cause," all of these obligations cease.

For simplicity we initially assume that they are all independent of attendance. Finally wage costs, for the most part, are paid only to workers actually working, hence the appropriate cost function becomes

$$[w_1 + (r + q)T]M + w_2\,aM\bar{H} + w_2\,baM(H - \bar{H}) \tag{2.6}$$

Through a simple transformation of variables, it is easy to see directly what the effect of the certainty absentee rate is on the equilibrium values of men and hours. Let $A = aM$, the number of employees actually working on a given day. Then rewriting formulas (2.6) and (2.7) the firm seeks to

$$\text{minimize} \quad [(w_1 + (r + q)T)/a]A + w_2\,A\bar{H} + w_2\,bA(H - \bar{H}) \tag{2.7}$$

$$\text{subject to} \quad L = F(A, H) \tag{2.8}$$

Obviously, in terms of the optimal (A, H) combination, a decrease in a (an increase in the absentee rate $1 - a$) has the same effect as an increase in any of the other components of costs that are independent of hours (w_0). That is, an increase in absenteeism increases the marginal cost of labor through additional workers in attendance, relative to the marginal cost of labor through additional overtime. Consequently,

$$\frac{\partial H^*}{\partial(1 - a)} > 0, \qquad \frac{\partial A^*}{\partial(1 - a)} < 0 \tag{2.9}$$

An increase in absenteeism causes a substitution of additional overtime per man for workers in attendance. In general, however, we cannot predict the effect on the equilibrium employment stock. Since $A = aM$ we know that

$$\frac{\partial M^*}{\partial(1 - a)} = \frac{1}{a}\frac{\partial A}{\partial(1 - a)} - \frac{M}{a} \tag{2.10}$$

While an increase in absenteeism (a decrease in the attendance rate) causes a substitution effect which tends to decrease employment [the first term in equation (2.10)], it also causes a scale effect since more employees are now required to attain a given level of workers in attendance on any day. Because the substitution and scale effects work in opposite directions, it is impossible to predict what the net effect of a certainty absentee rate is on the optimal number of employees.

Note that the above results will continue to hold even if some of the fixed employment costs, such as daily travel expenses, need not be paid to absentees. Similarly, they will hold if some (or all) absentees receive sick-leave payments. All that we crucially require is that absentees do *not* receive any pay for overtime hours that they may have been scheduled to work, and that some of the employment costs which are independent of hours worked are also independent of attendance. Let $\theta < 1$ be the proportion of absentees who receive sick leave (only for straight-time hours). Let $\gamma < 1$ be the proportion of fixed employment costs which must be paid for absent workers. The imputed turnover costs, $(r + q)T$, must be paid for the whole work force. Then the appropriate cost function is

$$w_1 M[a + (1 - a)\gamma] + (r + q)TM + w_2 M\bar{H}[a + (1 - a)\theta] + w_2 baM(H - \bar{H}) \tag{2.11}$$

This can be rewritten, in terms of workers in attendance as

$$\{w_1[a + (1 - a)\gamma] + (r + q)T\}A/a + w_2 A\bar{H}[a + (1 - a)\theta]/a + w_2 bA(H - \bar{H}) \tag{2.12}$$

The respective marginal costs of an additional worker in attendance and an additional hour of work for all workers in attendance are

$$MC_A = \{w_1[a + (1 - a)\gamma] + (r + q)T + w_2 \bar{H}[a + (1 - a)\theta]\}/a + w_2 b(H - \bar{H}) \tag{2.13}$$

$$MC_H = w_2 bA \tag{2.14}$$

For a given value of hours per worker (H) and workers in attendance, a change in the attendance rate (a) does not effect the marginal cost of an additional hour of work for all workers. On the other hand

$$\frac{\partial MC_A}{\partial a} = -[w_1 \gamma + w_2 \theta\bar{H} + (r + q)T]/a^2 < 0 \tag{2.15}$$

Since an increase in the *absentee* rate therefore increases the marginal cost of workers in attendance relative to that of additional hours per worker, a substitution of hours for workers in attendance takes place, i.e.,

$$\frac{\partial H^*}{\partial(1 - a)} > 0 \tag{2.16}$$

Hence as long as absentees are not paid for overtime, an increase in the certainty absentee rate will result in increased overtime hours per man. For notational convenience we assume $\theta = 0$, $\gamma = 1$; however, this simplification in no way affects the results which follow.

Instead of being known with certainty, we now assume that the attendance rate is a random variable with a probability density $p(a)$ that is symmetric around the variables mean value, $E(a)$. As in the recent works of K. Smith [63] [64] and M. Rothschild [60], we assume that the firm faces a two-stage decision process: the employer must choose the employment stock (M) each period before the actual realized value of the attendance rate is known. Once the attendance rate is observed, the level of hours per man (H) is determined from the labor services function (2.5) in order to meet production schedules. In view of our discussion in the opening paragraph of this section, the two-stage decision process seems particularly relevant in this context.

It is easy to illustrate graphically that, due to the assumption of diminishing marginal rate of substitution between workers in attendance and hours per worker, random fluctuation of absenteeism about a given mean level serves to *increase* the optimal stock of employees.

Referring to Figure 2–1, the contour $L = L_0$ indicates the various combinations of workers in attendance and hours per worker which yield the required level of labor services (L_0). Suppose that when absenteeism was nonstochastic that the equilibrium was given by the combination $[E(a)M^*, H^*]$. Now if the attendance rate is stochastic, symmetric fluctuations in worker attendance about $E(a)M^*$ (of size δ for example) will require compensating fluctuations in hours per worker. However, because of the assumed diminishing marginal rate of substitution, negative deviations in attendance require more than proportional increases in hours, while positive deviations require less than proportional increases (in Figure 2–1, $\varepsilon_2 > \varepsilon_1$). As a result, if the attendance rate is distributed symmetric about its mean, average hours associated with M^* in the stochastic case (H_u^*) will exceed the level of the certainty case (H^*). If we assume that the objective of the firm is to minimize the expected value of labor costs, then since $[E(a)M^*, H^*]$ represented the point at which the extensive (employee) marginal labor cost was equated to the intensive (hours/worker) marginal labor cost, we know that $[E(a)M^*, H_u^*]$ cannot be an equilibrium point. Effectively the intensive marginal cost has increased relative to the extensive marginal cost; for a given number of men, a larger number of hours per man are required on average. Consequently, it is optimal to *increase* the number of employees to some level $\hat{M} > M^*$. (Repetition of this type of argument obviously yields the conclusion that the optimal number of employees *increases* as the variability of the attendance rate increases.)

Associated with this employment level ($\hat{M}$), there is an optimal level of

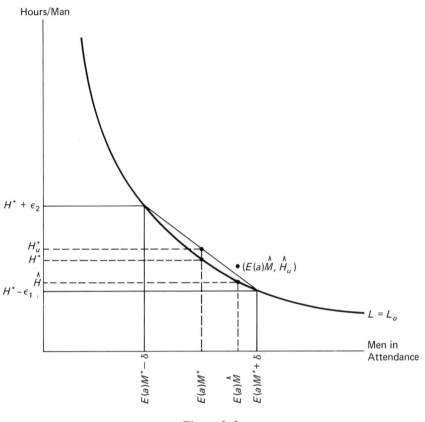

Figure 2-1.

the expected value of hours per man ($\hat{H}_u$). Due to the stochastic absentee rate and assumption of diminishing marginal rate of substitution between factors, $\hat{H}_u$ is greater than the level of hours per man that would be associated with $\hat{M}$ in the nonstochastic case ($\hat{H}$). While it is certainly true that $\hat{H} < H^*$ and $\hat{H} < H_u^*$, the relevant comparison is between $\hat{H}_u$ and H^*. That is, would we observe on average, a greater or smaller level of overtime per man in the stochastic or nonstochastic case? Figure 2-1 does not give us sufficient information to answer this question and indeed we have been unable to compare these terms for the general class of labor input functions in equation (2.5).

It appears that the comparison will depend upon properties of the labor input function, such as the elasticity of substitution between the factors, which determine the shape of the isoquant $L = L_0$.

If we consider the special case of the Cobb–Douglas labor input function, we can however uniquely determine the relationship between equilibrium over-time hours per man in the certainty and stochastic cases. That is, we assume

$$L = (aM)^{\alpha}H^{\beta} \qquad \alpha > \beta \qquad (2.17)$$

The requirement $\alpha > \beta$ is the second-order necessary condition corresponding to (2.2b) in the general case. (This condition will be crucial to what follows).

In addition to its analytic convenience, we may also justify the use of function (2.17) because it has been employed with success in recent empirical work ([23], [51]). For this particular function, the solution for equilibrium hours in the case of a certainty absentee rate of $E(a)$ becomes

$$H_c^* = \left[\frac{w_0 + (w_2 - w_2 b)\overline{H}E(a)}{w_2 bE(a)}\right]\left(\frac{\beta}{\alpha - \beta}\right) \qquad (2.18)$$

In the stochastic case, the firm knows that once it chooses an employment level M, hours per man will be uniquely determined by the value of the absentee rate that actually obtains in the period, i.e.,

$$H = L^{1/\beta}(aM)^{-\alpha/\beta} \qquad (2.19)$$

We assume that the firm will attempt to choose M, conditional on the value of H in equation (2.19), to minimize the expected value of its labor costs. Symbolically, substituting equation (2.19) into formula (2.6), the firm seeks to

$$\underset{\substack{M \\ a}}{\text{minimize}} \quad E\left[w_0 M + (w_2 - w_2 b)\overline{H}aM + w_2 bL^{1/\beta}(aM)^{(\beta - \alpha)/\beta}\right] \qquad (2.20)$$

The necessary condition for this unconstrained minimization problem is that

$$\underset{a}{E}\left[w_0 + (w_2 - w_2 b)\overline{H}a + \left(\frac{\beta - \alpha}{\beta}\right)w_2 bL^{1/\beta}a^{(\beta - \alpha)/\beta}M^{-\alpha/\beta}\right] = 0 \qquad (2.21)$$

or that

$$M^{-\alpha/\beta} = \frac{[w_0 + (w_2 - w_2 b)E(a)\overline{H}]}{w_2 \, bL^{1/\beta} \, E[a^{(\beta - \alpha)/\beta}]} \left(\frac{\beta}{\alpha - \beta}\right) \tag{2.22}$$

Substituting equation (2.22) into equation (2.19) when the attendance rate takes its mean value $E(a)$, determines the optimal expected level of hours per man in the stochastic case

$$H_u^* = \left[\frac{w_0 + (w_2 - w_2 b)E(a)\overline{H}}{w_2 \, bE[a^{(\beta - \alpha)/\beta}]}\right] [E(a)]^{-\alpha/\beta} \left(\frac{\beta}{\alpha - \beta}\right) \tag{2.23}$$

The optimal expected level of hours per man in the certainty (H_c^*) and stochastic (H_u^*) cases may now be directly compared. Dividing equation (2.18) by (2.23) results in

$$\frac{H_c^*}{H_u^*} = \frac{E[a^{(\beta - \alpha)/\beta}]}{[E(a)]^{(\beta - \alpha)/\beta}} \tag{2.24}$$

Since $\alpha > \beta$ is a necessary condition for our solution in equation (2.18) to be a relative minimum, we can let $\alpha = K\beta$, where $K > 1$, and obtain

$$\frac{H_c^*}{H_u^*} = \frac{E(a^{1-K})}{[E(a)]^{1-K}} \tag{2.25a}$$

or, rewriting,

$$\left(\frac{H_u^*}{H_c^*}\right)^{1/(K-1)} = \frac{[E(a^{1-K})]^{1/(1-K)}}{E(a)} \tag{2.25b}$$

Using Holder's inequality, it can be shown that the right-hand side of equation (2.25b) is always less than unity and hence, $H_u^* < H_c^*$.[13]

For this labor input function, the expected level of overtime per man is *less* in the stochastic absentee rate case, than when the absence rate is known with certainty.

---

[13] See [32], pp. 134–145, for a statement and proof of Holder's inequality and relevant corollaries. In particular it is shown that for any real number t, $[E(x^t)]^{1/t}$ is a monotonically increasing function of t. Note that if we define variability in terms of a "mean preserving spread," then Rothschild and Stiglitz [61], have shown that for any convex function $F(a)$, the expected value $E[F(a)]$ rises when the variability increases. Since a^{1-K} is convex for $K > 1$, it immediately follows from equation (2.24) that an increase in variability decreases the optimal level of overtime per man.

Summarizing the results of this section briefly, contrary to popular belief it is not always the stochastic nature of absenteeism which is responsible for increased overtime hours per man above the zero absentee level. A certainty absentee rate modifies the labor cost function in a nonsymmetric way so as to increase the marginal cost of labour purchased through additional workers relative to the marginal cost of labor purchased through increased hours per man and consequently induces a substitution of hours per man for workers. The net effect on the employment stock is ambiguous, however, since the scale effect of increased absenteeism tends to increase employment. A stochastic absentee rate tends to increase the optimal employment level above that of the certainty absentee rate case. While the effect on the expected level of hours per man has not been determined in general, for the special case of the Cobb–Douglas labor input function it is shown that the optimal level decreases. That is, observed overtime hours per man would be lower in the stochastic than the nonstochastic case.

A Dynamic Model and the Problem of Disequilibrium Bias

The equilibrium positions determined by the static models of the previous section can be thought of as the stationary equilibrium solutions that are embedded in underlying dynamic models. If all firms are in stationary equilibrium, as is customarily assumed in cross-section econometric work, then any two firms which face identical sets of parameters will be observed to have identical levels of hours of work per man. On the other hand, if firms are *not* all in stationary equilibrium, but rather spaced along the dynamic adjustment paths derived from the dynamic models, then two firms which face identical parameters may be observed to have different levels of hours per man. Unless we can take account of this latter possibility our econometric results will be difficult to interpret. To illustrate more precisely the problems involved, the remainder of this section heuristically outlines a simple dynamic model that combines some of the ideas found in Solow [67] and Treadway [69].

We consider a model of a single-plant, single-product firm with a homogeneous labor force. The rate of change of the firm's employment stock ($\dot{M}$) is given by

$$\dot{M} = AC - LY - OS \qquad (2.26a)$$

Here AC is the number of accessions, LY is the number of employees laid off, and OS is the number of " other separations " (primarily quits and other voluntary separations). Assuming, as in the previous sections, that this latter category is a constant proportion (q) of the firm's stock of employees, the identity can be rewritten as

$$\dot{M} + qM = AC - LY \qquad (2.26b)$$

As noted previously, accessions and layoffs are not costless.[14] Recruiting, hiring, and training costs must be incurred for accessions; while those laid off often receive severance pay or supplementary unemployment compensation benefits. In addition substantial real losses of output may occur due to high turnover in periods of either rapid expansion or contraction.[15] Given that costs exist in both hiring and laying off employees, it can be easily demonstrated that a rational firm will never both hire and lay off workers at the same time and consequently,

$$N = \dot{M} + qM \qquad (2.26c)$$

where

$$N = \begin{cases} AC & \text{if } AC > 0 \quad \text{and} \quad LY = 0 \\ LY & \text{if } LY > 0 \quad \text{and} \quad AC = 0. \end{cases}$$

The costs associated with adjusting the labor stock are assumed to satisfy

$$C(N) \geq 0, \qquad C(0) = 0, \qquad C' \gtreqless 0 \quad \text{as} \quad N \gtreqless 0, \qquad C'' > 0$$

This turnover cost function will not in general be symmetric about the zero level of turnovers, since the costs involved in accessions and separations are not the same. Note also that in the previous sections, the marginal cost of turnover (C') was assumed constant at the level T. Without this constancy, the invariance of hours to scale in stationary equilibrium will not hold. Since our econometric work will not be based on this model, this property will not concern us here.

Given an initial stock of employees, stationary expectations on all the

---

[14] Many of these costs are enumerated in detail in Soligo [66]. Holt et al. [35], Becker [6], and Oi [52] were among the first to incorporate these costs into economic analysis.

[15] See Soligio [66], p. 174.

exogenously given cost parameters, and a required level of labor services that is expected to exist indefinitely, the firm is assumed to choose the time paths of its employment stock and hours per employee in an attempt to minimize the present value of its labor costs. Symbolically, the problem is to

$$\text{minimize} \int_0^\infty \{w_1 M + w_2 M\bar{H} + w_2 bM(H - \bar{H}) + C(N)\}e^{-rt}\,dt \quad (2.27)$$

$$\text{subject to} \quad M_0 = \bar{M}_0 \quad\quad\quad\quad\quad\quad\quad\quad (2.27a)$$

$$\bar{L} = F(M, H) \quad\quad\quad\quad\quad\quad\quad (2.27b)$$

$$N = \dot{M} + qM \quad\quad\quad\quad\quad\quad\quad (2.27c)$$

We are ignoring absenteeism here and considering behavior only in a neighborhood of equilibrium. In particular, this formulation assumes that the entire solution path lies in the overtime region; this assumption is not necessary for the results that follow. The notation is the same as that of the previous sections.

This problem can be solved using the classical calculus of variations. For brevity, we omit the actual derivation of the solution here and consider only the relevant results. The gross rate of change of the firm's employment stock (N) is seen to be a function of the stock of employees at each point in time and all the parameters in the model. That is,

$$N = N(M, w_1, w_2, b, \bar{H}, q, r, L) \quad\quad\quad (2.28)$$

The parameters of the turnover cost function should also be included as an argument of this function.

For two firms which face identical labor-service requirements and cost parameters, this reduces to

$$N = N(M) \quad \text{where} \quad N'(M) < 0 \quad\quad\quad (2.29)$$

The solution path for the gross rate of change of employment is illustrated in Figure 2–2a. If initially an employment stock of $\bar{M}$ is held, the firm should hire enough new employees to achieve an instantaneous rate of increase of employment of $\bar{N}$. Figure 2–2a shows then, the change in employment to be optimally associated with each level of employment as the firm moves towards equilibrium. At equilibrium (M^*), new hires are just equal to replacements (qM^*). Crucially, as long as the turnover cost function is convex ($C'' > 0$), adjustment to equilibrium will *not* be instantaneous, but rather will follow a path similar to that illustrated in Figure 2–2a.

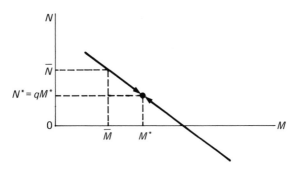

Figure 2-2a.

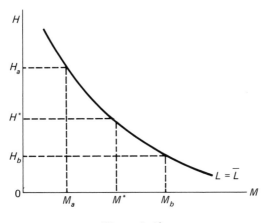

Figure 2-2b.

If adjustment to stationary equilibrium is not instantaneous, firms facing identical cost parameters, but with different initial stocks of men, will be spaced along the dynamic adjustment path. However, given a fixed level of labor services $(\bar{L})$, the labor requirements function (2–27b) can be inverted and hours per man uniquely related to the level of employment. In particular, given the assumptions (2.29) and (2.2b) we have,

$$H = H(M), \qquad H' < 0, \quad \text{and} \quad H'' > 0 \tag{2.30}$$

A representative isoquant is drawn in Figure 2–2b and serves to illustrate the problem that we face. In stationary equilibrium, hours per man are determined by the various cost parameters. However given $\bar{L}$, hours per man are uniquely determined along the adjustment path by the stock of men present at each point in time. Consequently, if firms are not all in stationary equilibrium, observed hours per man may vary even if they all face *identical* cost parameters and labor-service requirements. Unless we can account for this variation, caused by firms being spaced along the dynamic adjustment path, our econometric results will be difficult to interpret. One of the tasks of the next chapter is to provide a solution to this problem.

3

Heterogeneous Labor, the Internal Labor Market, and the Dynamics of the Employment-Hours Decision

Introduction

In an attempt to build a realistic theoretical model to serve as the basis for our empirical work, this chapter relaxes several of the assumptions of the previous chapter that are obviously contradicted by empirical evidence. We also attempt to explicitly include a few institutional features of unionized labor markets into the model since we believe that it is more appropriate to incorporate such features directly into theoretical models before deriving testable implications, rather than invoking their presence to "explain" anomalies in empirical results based on tests of a competitive neoclassical model. Consequently, in this chapter we introduce such concepts as heterogeneous labor, the internal labor market, and the establishment wage structure into a model designed to explain the dynamics of the employment-hours decisions. Among the questions we seek to answer is why not all employees of a given establishment work the same amount of overtime and more specifically, is it ever rational for management to agree to union demands that overtime be scheduled on the basis of seniority? We also can explicitly indicate how our cross-section empirical results will be affected by firms being in short-run equilibrium along the dynamic equilibrium adjustment path derived from the model, instead of all being in long-run stationary equilibrium. This is seen to be an aggregation problem, which is solvable due to the assumptions of the model.

We will first discuss more explicitly the motivation for this chapter, while the next section introduces the assumptions and notation for the model. The model is formulated, the necessary conditions interpreted, and the comparative static and dynamic results described in the next three sections. We then discuss and solve the aggregation problem; it is seen that the solution implies the need to utilize simultaneous equation methods when seeking to explain cross-section intraindustry variations in observed overtime hours per man. The final section serves as a brief conclusion.

[1] The results derived in this chapter have been presented in a slightly different form in my paper of the same title published in the *Journal of Economic Theory*, 3, March 1971: 85–104.

Motivation

Inspection of various Bureau of Labor Statistics' publications indicates that our previous assumption of a unique hourly wage rate and fringe costs per man in any single establishment is patently false. The number of weeks of paid vacation a year to which an employee is entitled is usually positively related to his seniority, with new employees receiving no vacations.[2] New employees, in addition, are not always immediately eligible for holiday pay and many privately established welfare benefits such as health insurance and pension coverage.[3] The period of employment required for eligibility extends to over a year in some cases. Besides receiving lower fringe benefits, new workers also receive lower wages than senior workers performing the same task.[4] In sum, our average cost observations do not represent the marginal costs of new employees and this fact should be accounted for in our theoretical model.

Previous models of labor demand, such as that of Solow [67], often implicitly assume that labor is homogeneous. However, labor is not homogeneous, but heterogeneous, if only because of skill differentials due to learning by doing or on-the-job training. In some crafts, specific apprenticeship programs are established; in others, training is less formal. In either case, it is reasonable to assume that in addition to having lower costs, new workers usually have lower productivity than other workers.

Evidence also indicates that all workers in a given establishment do not work the same amount of overtime. Union rules often require that overtime be assigned on the basis of seniority.[5] While a theoretical model might be built which restricts overtime to being assigned in such a manner,[6] it is more interesting to ask how employers would allocate overtime in the absence of such rules, and subsequently ask, does management act rationally in agreeing to the imposition of such rules?

The concept of an internal labor market and seniority structure are important in many unionized industries. Promotion among production workers is primarily from within the establishment, with jobs awarded on an "ability" basis to those from the eligible seniority class. If job classifications can be thought of as rungs of a ladder, in the extreme case the only

---

[2] See the various B.L.S. *Wage Chronologies* [81].

[3] See B.L.S. Bulletin 1502, *Digest of 100 Selected Health and Insurance Plans under Collective Bargaining Early 1966* [82].

[4] B.L.S. *Wage Chronologies*.

[5] See *Overtime Pay Penalty Act of 1964* [70].

[6] M. G. Orrbeck et al. [53] constructed a dynamic programming model in which it was assumed that overtime was assigned strictly on the basis of seniority.

"port of entry" from the external market is at the lowest rung.[7] That is, new hires occur only in the lowest classification. Similarly, layoffs are governed by seniority. Those without seniority can be laid off at essentially almost zero cost, however, with the various supplementary unemployment benefit, guaranteed annual wage, and severance pay plans, it becomes expensive to lay off senior workers.[8] A realistic model of firm behavior should take account of these institutional facts.

Once we incorporate all of the above features into a dynamic model of firm behavior, we can answer questions about several problems that arise when equations seeking to explain interfirm variations in observed overtime hours per man are estimated: Can we account for the fact that different classes of workers within a firm work differing amounts of overtime, when we can only observe the average for all employees of the firm? What if firms are not all in long-run equilibrium? If it is optimal to vary the hours of any class along the dynamic adjustment path, how will this affect interfirm cross-section regressions? If it is optimal to vary the ratio of new to senior workers along the equilibrium path, how will this affect the observed values of over-time across firms? These questions are all part of a general aggregation problem, which we are able to solve explicitly for the model presented in this chapter.

Notation and Assumptions of the Model

We consider a model with two different classes of employees, "new" workers (M_1) and "senior" workers (M_2). All employees within a class are homogeneous and the members of each class work H_1 and H_2 hours per man per week respectively. The two classes have constant proportional quit rates of q_1 and q_2 respectively. Through an argument similar to Becker [6], we could argue that due to specific training, nonvested pensions, and the seniority structure in general, new workers will probably have a higher quit rate than senior workers. However, this is inessential to what follows and indeed it will turn out that the analytics of the model are independent of the value of q_1.

We assume that the wage rates, fringe-benefit costs, the wage structure, and "normal" hours of work are given to the firm by collective bargaining or some other means. For simplicity we assume that for both classes of workers, after $\bar{H}$ hours of work per week, an overtime premium must be paid. Since

---

[7] See Clark Kerr, "The Balkanization of Labor Markets," in Bakke [38].

[8] See B.L.S. Bulletin [83], [85], [86] among others. Also Becker [7]. Specific training costs invested in senior workers also increase the costs of laying them off. See Becker [6] and Oi [52].

$\bar{H}$ is determined either through collective bargaining or through the Fair Labor Standards Act, there is no obvious reason to assume that it is equal to the optimal levels of H_1 and H_2 which employers would choose in the short-run. We will explicitly assume throughout, in fact, that equilibrium for both classes is in the overtime region.[9]

Let w_1 be the fixed costs per senior worker. These are the costs per week per employee which are independent of the exact number of hours that he works and include a large portion of fringe-benefit costs. Let w_2 and bw_2 be respectively the hourly wage rate and overtime wage rate (b is greater than unity) for senior workers. We argued in the previous section that costs are lower for new workers, hence we assume that γ_1 and γ_2 (both less than one) are the proportion of senior workers' fixed costs and wage rate respectively that new workers receive.

We assume that the flow of labor services (L) that the firm receives is given by

$$L = M_1\beta(H_1) + KM_2\beta(H_2) \qquad K > 1, \quad \beta' > 0, \quad \beta'' < 0 \qquad (3.1)$$

Since the form of this function is essential for the results that follow, it is appropriate to derive it here somewhat rigorously. In general, if a firm employs n workers, the flow of labor services it receives will be some general function of the number of hours (h_i) that each man works.

$$L = F(h_1, h_2, \ldots, h_n)$$

We now assume that this function is additively separable in its arguments. That is, changing the number of hours that employee i works does not effect the marginal contribution to labor services of an additional hour worked by employee j.

$$L = \sum_{i=1}^{n} \beta_i(h_i) \Rightarrow \frac{\partial^2 L}{\partial h_i \partial h_j} = 0$$

We have previously assumed that employees can be divided into two classes. Since workers are homogeneous within classes, all workers in a given class will work the same number of hours. Assume that each of the first M_1 workers, the new workers, has productivity given by $\beta(H_1)$, where H_1 is the number of hours per week that each new employee works. Assume that each

---

[9] With only slight modifications in the analysis, the case when equilibrium for only one class is in the overtime region can be easily handled.

of the remaining M_2 workers ($M_1 + M_2 = n$), the senior workers, is K times as productive as each new worker (if both classes worked the same number of hours per man). Then the labor input function may be written as

$$L = \sum_{i=1}^{M_1} \beta(H_1) + \sum_{i=M_1+1}^{M_1+M_2} K\beta(H_2)$$

This aggregates to (1) of course. The properties on β express the familiar notion that an increase in the number of hours worked per man will increase labor services but at a diminishing rate (perhaps due to the effects of fatigue). Again if both new and senior workers work the same number of hours, then K is the relative productivity advantage of senior workers over new workers and this advantage is independent of the number of either class of workers that are employed.[10]

We will assume that the firm requires a constant flow of labor services ($\bar{L}$) over time. This is less restrictive than assuming a constant output requirement, since we can invert the neoclassical production function $Q = F(S, L, T)$ to get

$$\overset{+ \;\; - \;\; -}{L = G(Q, S, T)} \tag{3.2}$$

Here Q is output, S is capital services, and T the level of technology.[11] The sign over the variables in equation (3.2) indicates the sign of the relevant partial. Hence output may indeed be increasing over time as long as the level of technology and capital services compensatingly increase. Such a combination would lead to an increasing output–labor ratio over time which is consistent with rough empirical evidence.

To introduce the notion of the internal labor market, we make the strict assumption that layoffs and new hires can occur only in the class of new workers. Morever we assume that the costs of hiring and laying off new workers are basically zero (as compared to the training costs which will be introduced in a moment) and can be ignored. This essentially means that we can act as if the stock of new employees (M_1) is freely chosen each period.

---

[10] In Chapter 2, we worked with both the general labor input function $F(M, H)$ and the special case $M^\alpha H^\beta$. When $\alpha = 1$, the latter is obviously a special case of the function used here.

[11] The form of the production function assumes a "nested" labor input function. This rules out the possibility of the different classes of labor having differing partial elasticities of substitution with capital.

New employees must undergo training to increase their productivity before they achieve seniority status. The amount of training required is assumed to be fixed, since K is assumed constant. However, the length of the training period may be varied. The shorter the training period, the more intensive the training must be within the period, and hence the greater the instantaneous marginal cost of training each new employee per period. In fact it is probably reasonable to assume that this cost increases at an increasing rate. If we let $1/\theta$ be the average period that new workers must spend in training before achieving seniority, then θ will be the average proportion of new workers that achieve seniority at each moment in time. Since no new hires or layoffs can occur in the class of senior workers, the net flow of workers into senior status during a small period of length dt is given by

$$M_2(t) - M_2(t - dt) = \theta\, dt[1 - q_1\, dt]M_1(t - dt) - q_2\, dt\, M_2(t - dt)$$

Dividing both sides by dt and then taking the limit as dt approaches zero, we obtain

$$\dot{M}_2 = \theta M_1 - q_2 M_2 \tag{3.3}$$

As noted above θ is a decision variable for the firm, and the costs of training can be represented as follows (remembering that an increase in θ is equivalent to decreasing the length of the training period).

$$c(\theta)M_1 \qquad c'(\theta) > 0 \qquad c''(\theta) > 0 \qquad \infty > \theta > 0$$

Several limitations of the model should be indicated here. We are assuming that only new workers receive training. New workers' productivity jumps instantaneously when they achieve seniority; a gradual increase in productivity could be introduced only at the expense of introducing a continuum of classes of employees. New workers are "forgetful" in the sense that any new worker who does not achieve seniority at a point in time but is rehired, must undergo training again. Finally, it is assumed that the period necessary to achieve seniority is equal to the period necessary to undergo training to increase productivity. Since the former is determined by collective bargaining this will not always be valid, however, it again seems impossible to relax this assumption without introducing at least an additional class of employees.

The Model

Given an initial stock of senior employees and static expectations on all of the parameters in the model, the firm is assumed to choose the time paths of

$H_1(t)$, $H_2(t)$, $M_1(t)$, $\dot{M}_2(t)$, and $\theta(t)$ to minimize the present value of its labor costs over an infinite horizon. That is, the firm problem is to

$$\text{minimize} \int_0^\infty e^{-rt} \frac{[w_1(\gamma_1 M_1 + M_2) + w_2(\gamma_2 M_1 \overline{H} + M_2 \overline{H})}{+ w_2 b[\gamma_2 M_1(H_1 - \overline{H}) + M_2(H_2 - \overline{H})] + c(\theta)M_1] dt}$$

subject to

$$M_2(0) = \overline{M}_{20}$$
$$\overline{L} = M_1 \beta(H_1) + M_2 K\beta(H_2)$$
$$\dot{M}_2 = \theta M_1 - q_2 M_2$$
$$H_1 > \overline{H}, \quad H_2 > \overline{H}, \quad \theta > 0$$

This problem can be solved using the classical calculus of variations.[12] Letting λ_1 and λ_2 be multipliers, the problem can be formulated as seeking to minimize the integral of the following expression:

$$J = e^{-rt}\{w_1(\gamma_1 M_1 + M_2) + w_2 \overline{H}(\gamma_2 M_1 + M_2) + w_2 b[\gamma_2 M_1(H_1 - \overline{H})$$
$$+ M_2(H_2 - \overline{H})] + c(\theta)M_1 + \lambda_1(\dot{M}_2 - \theta M_1 + q_2 M_2) \quad (3.4)$$
$$+ \lambda_2[L - M_1\beta(_1)H - KM_2\beta(H_2)]\}$$

The time paths of the variables that minimize the above must satisfy the following conditions.

Legendre

The Legendre necessary condition essentially requires that after explicitly substituting for M_2 in terms of M_1, H_1, H_2, and θ, the matrix of second partials

$$J_{X_I X_J} = \begin{bmatrix} J_{H_1 H_1} & & & \text{cross} \\ & & & \text{partials} \\ & J_{H_2 H_2} & & \\ \text{cross} & & J_{M_1 M_1} & \\ \text{partials} & & & \\ & & & J_{\theta\theta} \end{bmatrix}$$

---

[12] A readable account of the calculus of variations can be found in Gelfand and Fomin [30].

be positive semidefinite. It can be shown that $c'' > 0$ and $\beta'' < 0$ guarantee that this condition will be met.

Euler–Lagrange

$$w_2\, b\gamma_2\, M_1 - \lambda_2\, M_1 \beta'(H_1) = 0 \qquad (3.5a)$$

$$w_2\, bM_2 - \lambda_2\, M_2\, K\beta'(H_2) = 0 \qquad (3.5b)$$

$$w_1\gamma_1 + w_2\,\gamma_2\,\bar{H} + w_2\, b\gamma_2(H_1 - \bar{H}) + c(\theta) - \lambda_1\theta - \lambda_2\,\beta(H_1) = 0 \qquad (3.5c)$$

$$[w_1 + w_2\,\bar{H} + w_2\, b(H_2 - \bar{H}) + \lambda_1 q_2 - \lambda_2\, K\beta(H_2)]e^{-rt} = \frac{d}{dt}[e^{-rt}\lambda_1] \qquad (3.5d)$$

$$c'(\theta)M_1 - \lambda_1 M_1 = 0 \qquad (3.5e)$$

$$\dot{M}_2 = \theta M_1 - q_2\, M_2 \qquad (3.5f)$$

$$L = M_1\beta(H_1) + M_2\, K\beta(H_2) \qquad (3.5g)$$

Transversality

Along with the Euler conditions, the transversality condition is a sufficient condition, given the suitable convexity of the problem.

$$\lim_{t\to\infty} e^{-rt}\lambda_1 = 0 \qquad (3.5h)$$

The interpretation of these conditions is straightforward and yields several interesting results. For notational simplicity we will use the following symbols here:

MC = instantaneous marginal cost of a variable
MPP = instantaneous marginal contribution to labor services of a variable

Conditions (3.5a) and (3.5b) together yield the result that

$$\lambda_2 = \frac{MC_{H_1}}{MPP_{H_1}} = \frac{MC_{H_2}}{MPP_{H_2}} \tag{3.6}$$

This is the standard condition on completely variable factors expected from static theory. Solving it explicitly we find that

$$\beta'(H_1) = \gamma_2 K \beta'(H_2) \quad \text{or} \quad K \gtreqqless \frac{1}{\gamma_2} \Leftrightarrow H_2 \gtreqqless H_1 \tag{3.7}$$

Recall that K is the relative productivity advantage of senior workers, and that since γ_2 is the proportion of senior workers' hourly wage rate that new workers receive, $1/\gamma_2$ is the relative cost disadvantage of senior workers. Hence if the relative productivity advantage of senior workers is greater than their relative hourly cost disadvantage, it is rational to have them work longer hours.[13] Management may therefore be acting rationally in agreeing to union demands that overtime be assigned on the basis of seniority. Later we will indicate, in fact, a method by which we will be able to empirically determine the relationship between γ_2 and K.

From equation (3.5e) we see that λ_1 must be equal to the marginal cost per new worker of changing the flow into seniority status by changing the length of the training period $c'(\theta)$. Substituting this and equation (3.6) into (3.5c) we obtain

$$\theta c'(\theta) = MC_{M_1} - MC_{H_1} \frac{MPP_{M_1}}{MPP_{H_1}} \tag{3.8}$$

Only if $\theta = 0$ would we have the static condition that the ratio of the instantaneous marginal costs be equated to the rate of technical substitution between the two variables. In fact, the length of the training period $(1/\theta)$ must be finite and positive and consequently θ is always positive. Thus we have the conclusion that

$$\frac{MC_{M_1}}{MPP_{M_1}} > \frac{MC_{H_1}}{MPP_{H_1}} \tag{3.8a}$$

---

[13] This conclusion utilizes the assumption $\beta'' < 0$.

This result is easy to comprehend once we recall the institutional features of our model. The only way to obtain senior employees is to first hire them as new workers. When we consider only the instantaneous marginal costs and marginal contribution to labor services of new employees, we include their training costs but ignore their future increases in productivity and thus the inequality (3.8a) results. Moreover, by substituting (3.5b), (3.5c), and (3.8) into (3.5d), we can then integrate to find that the time paths of the decision variables must be chosen such that[14]

$$c'[\theta(t)] = \int_t^\infty e^{-r(T-\tau)} \left\{ \left[MC_{M_2} - MC_{H_2} \frac{MPP_{M_2}}{MPP_{H_2}} \right] \right.$$
$$\left. + \frac{q_2}{\theta} \left[MC_{M_1} - MC_{H_1} \frac{MPP_{M_1}}{MPP_{H_1}} \right] \right\} dT \quad (3.9)$$

Note that in stationary equilibrium $q_2 M_2 = \theta M_1$. Thus the term q_2/θ can be looked upon as a long-run multiplier that indicates the equilibrium ratio of new to senior workers. Assuming that we are initially in long-run equilibrium, we can explicitly integrate equation (3.9) to obtain (after substitution)

$$c'(\theta)(r + q_2) = MC_{H_2} \frac{MPP_{M_2}}{MPP_{H_2}} - MC_{M_2} \quad (3.9a)$$

or, in long-run equilibrium,

$$\frac{MC_{H_2}}{MPP_{H_2}} > \frac{MC_{M_2}}{MPP_{M_2}} \quad (3.10)$$

Again this inequality is understandable since the instantaneous marginal cost of senior workers ignores the cost of training new workers to replace those who quit from the pool of senior workers. Indeed (3.6), (3.8a), and (3.10) together yield that in long-run equilibrium, since future increases in productivity are not included in the instantaneous marginal calculations,

$$\frac{MC_{M_1}}{MPP_{M_1}} > \frac{MC_{M_2}}{MPP_{M_2}} \quad (3.10a)$$

---

[14] The time index of all of the variables on the right-hand side is suppressed for notational simplicity.

The transversality condition (3.5h) states that the discounted marginal cost per man of the training period should approach zero as time approaches infinity. This essentially requires that the training period $1/\theta$ not exponentially decrease forever at a rate greater than the interest rate r. A constant training period or a path that approaches a constant θ will obviously satisfy this condition. Finally conditions (3.5f) and (3.5g) repeat the labor-services constraint and the constraint which determines the flow of workers into senior status.

Comparative Statics of the Model

Before considering the dynamics of the system, we initially assume that a stationary long-run equilibrium with $\dot{M}_2 = \dot{\theta} = 0$ exists. Then the dynamic system (3.5a to 3.5g) can be reduced to the following five-equation static system with M_1^*, M_2^*, H_1^*, H_2^*, θ^* as long-run decision variables.

$$\theta^* M_1^* - q_2 M_2^* = 0 \tag{3.11a}$$

$$M_1^* \beta(H_1^*) + K M_2^* \beta(H_2^*) = L \tag{3.11b}$$

$$\beta'(H_1^*) - \gamma_2 K \beta'(H_2^*) = 0 \tag{3.11c}$$

$$w_1 \gamma_1 + w_2(1-b)\gamma_2 \overline{H} + w_2 b \gamma_2 \left[H_1^* - \frac{\beta(H_1^*)}{\beta'(H_1^*)} \right] + c(\theta^*) - \theta^* c'(\theta^*) = 0 \tag{3.11d}$$

$$w_1 + w_2(1-b)\overline{H} + w_2 b \left(H_2^* - \frac{\beta(H_2^*)}{\beta'(H_2^*)} \right) + (r + q_2)c'(\theta^*) = 0 \tag{3.11e}$$

To obtain qualitative implications as to the effect of a change in any parameter on the equilibrium values of the variables, we take the total differential of the system and obtain in matrix form,[15]

---

[15] For notational simplicity we omit the * superscript which refers to long-run equilibrium values. Throughout this section we are considering only such positions.

$$
\begin{bmatrix}
\theta & 0 & -q_2 & 0 & M_1 \\
\beta(H_1) & M_1\beta'(H_1) & K\beta(H_2) & KM_2\beta'(H_2) & 0 \\
0 & \beta''(H_1) & 0 & -\gamma_2 K\beta''(H_2) & 0 \\
0 & \dfrac{w_2 b\gamma_2\beta(H_1)\beta''(H_1)}{[\beta'(H_1)]^2} & 0 & 0 & -\theta c'' \\
0 & 0 & 0 & \dfrac{w_2 b\beta(H_2)\beta''(H_2)}{(\beta'(H_2))^2} & (r+q_2)c''
\end{bmatrix}
\begin{bmatrix}
dM_1 \\ dH_1 \\ dM_2 \\ dH_2 \\ d\theta
\end{bmatrix}
$$

$$
=
$$

$$
\begin{bmatrix}
0 & 0 & 0 & 0 & 0 & 0 & M_2 & 0 & 0 & 0 \\
0 & 0 & 0 & 0 & 0 & 0 & 0 & -M_2\beta(H_2) & 0 & 1 \\
0 & 0 & 0 & 0 & 0 & K\beta'(H_2) & 0 & \gamma_2\beta'(H_2) & 0 & 0 \\
-\gamma_1 & x_1 & (b-1)\gamma_2 w_2 & y_1 & -w_1 & x_1\dfrac{w_2}{y_2} & 0 & 0 & 0 & 0 \\
-1 & x_2 & (b-1)w_2 & y_2 & 0 & 0 & -c'(\theta) & 0 & -c'(\theta) & 0
\end{bmatrix}
\begin{bmatrix}
dw_1 \\ dw_2 \\ d\bar{H} \\ d\gamma_1 \\ d\gamma_2 \\ dq_2 \\ dK \\ dr \\ dL
\end{bmatrix}
$$

$$(3.12\text{a})$$

where the conditions $\beta(0) = 0$, $\beta' > 0$, and $\beta'' < 0$ are sufficient to guarantee that x_1, x_2, y_1, and y_2 are all positive, and

$$
x_1 = b\gamma_2\left[\frac{\beta(H_1)}{\beta'(H_1)} - H_1\right] + (b-1)\gamma_2\bar{H} > 0 \tag{3.12b}
$$

$$
x_2 = b\left[\frac{\beta(H_2)}{\beta'(H_2)} - H_2\right] + (b-1)\bar{H} > 0 \tag{3.12c}
$$

$$
y_1 = w_2\gamma_2\left[\frac{\beta(H_1)}{\beta'(H_1)} - H_1\right] + w_2\gamma_2\bar{H} > 0 \tag{3.12d}
$$

$$
y_2 = w_2\left[\frac{\beta(H_2)}{\beta'(H_2)} - H_2\right] + w_2\bar{H} > 0 \tag{3.12e}
$$

If we denote by D the determinant of the top matrix and let D_{ij} be the cofactor of the ith row and jth column of that matrix, then somewhat tedious calculation reveals that $D < 0$ and[16]

$$[D_{ij}] = \begin{bmatrix} - & 0 & + & 0 & 0 \\ - & 0 & - & 0 & 0 \\ + & + & a & - & - \\ - & + & ? & + & + \\ a & + & - & + & - \end{bmatrix} \qquad (3.12\text{f})$$

Using Cramer's Rule (see the appendix to this chapter) we are then able to determine the comparative statics of the model. In particular, the results tabulated below are obtained, where the sign in a square indicates the sign of the partial derivative of the variable with respect to the parameter.[17]

	∂w_1	∂w_2	$\partial \bar{H}$	∂b	$\partial \gamma_1$	$\partial \gamma_2$	∂q_2	∂K	∂r	∂L
∂H_1^*	+	−	−	−	+	−	+	−	+	0
∂H_2^*	+	−	−	−	+	?	+	+	+	0
∂M_1^*	?	?	?	?	−	?	?	−	?	+
∂M_2^*	?	?	?	?	?	?	−	?	−	+
$\partial \theta^*$	?	?	?	?	+	?	−	+	−	0

Since our primary empirical concern is with the determinants of overtime behavior, we first note that hours worked for both classes of workers are

---

[16] a means that D_{33} and D_{51} are negative if $H_1 > H_2(\gamma_2 K < 1)$, otherwise their signs are ambiguous.

[17] If $\gamma_2 K < 1$ then $\partial M_1/\partial r$, $\partial M_1/\partial w_1$, $\partial M_1/\partial q_2 < 0$ and $\partial M_1/\partial w_2$, $\partial M_1/\partial b$, $\partial M_1/\partial \bar{H} > 0$. This is true because for $x = r$, w_1, w_2, b, $\bar{H}$, or q_2,

(a) $\partial H_1/\partial x$, $\partial H_2/\partial x$ are of the same sign and this implies that at least one of $\partial M_1/\partial x$ and $\partial M_2/\partial x$ be of opposite sign.

(b) When $\gamma_2 K < 1$ then $D_{51} < 0$ and consequently

$$\frac{\partial}{\partial H_1}\left(\frac{\partial L}{\partial M_1}\right)\bigg/\frac{\partial L}{\partial M_1} < \frac{\partial}{\partial H_2}\left(\frac{\partial L}{\partial M_2}\right)\bigg/\frac{\partial L}{\partial M_2}$$

That is, whenever an increase in new employees' hours causes a smaller percentage increase in the marginal contribution to labor services of a new employee than does the corresponding increase in senior workers' hours cause in the marginal contribution to labor services of a senior employee then we should definitely decrease the number of new workers.

invariant with respect to desired labor services. An increase in the level of fixed costs, senior workers' quit rate, or the interest rate will all increase overtime for both classes. Similarly a decrease in the wage rate, overtime premium, or the level of standard hours will again increase overtime for both classes. These results are identical with our results in the previous chapter and can be easily understood on economic grounds. An increase in senior workers' productivity increases overtime of that class, while decreasing it for new workers. Finally an increase in the fixed costs of new workers increases overtime for both classes, while an increase in the relative wage rate of new workers decreases overtime for that class, the effect on senior workers' hours being ambiguous.

In those cases where the signs are unambiguous, the partials of the employment stocks are similar to those of our earlier work. However, in many cases the signs are indeterminate. Given the labor input constraint (3.11b), an increase in one variable (say M_1) need not imply a decrease in any specific one (say M_2) of the other three variables (in this case M_2, H_1, H_2). This is one source of the ambiguity since in the homogeneous labor case discussed in Chapter 2, an increase in hours (given L) *necessarily* implied a compensating decrease in the employment stock. Moreover, since θ is a decision variable, M_1 and M_2 are not necessarily uniquely positively related (given senior workers' quit rate) in the long run as might be expected from (3.11b). For example, an increase in K decreases M_1, but since it increases θ, need not also decrease M_2.[18] In any case, since we are primarily interested in the hours equations, these ambiguities do not disturb us.

One interesting "nonresult" should be noted, however. It has been argued that decreasing the wage rates of unskilled labor relative to those of skilled labor should increase the employment of the unskilled relative to the skilled. Studies of wage differentials, such as Hildebrand and Delehanty [33], find that, in spite of persistent high unemployment rates among unskilled workers, wage differentials have not widened appreciably over the postwar period. This may be attributed partially to minimum wages and partially to the fact that in some industries skilled and unskilled workers are not completely separate classes. That is, unskilled workers are often those employees entering from the external market at the bottom rung. Over time they achieve seniority, are promoted, and enter the skilled classification. Entry rates are therefore

---

[18] To illustrate the economic rationale for the various signs and ambiguities, we note that an increase in K has both scale and substitution effects. From (3.12g), the scale effect is zero for hours of both classes ($\partial H_1/\partial L$, $\partial H_2/\partial L = 0$) and hence their partials are unambiguous. The scale and substitution effects both tend to decrease M_1, but they act on opposite directions on M_2 (hence the ambiguity).

not free to vary completely independently of the rates of senior workers; an internal wage structure exists. What our model indicates however [see (3.12g)], is that even if it were free to be varied, a decrease in the relative wage rate of new workers (γ_2) would *not* unambiguously increase their employment. All that we can definitely say is that existing new workers would work longer hours.

Finally, we note that the length of the training period is also invariant to the level of desired labor services. An increase in the quit rate tends to increase the length of the training period (decrease θ) while an increase in the productivity of senior workers or the relative fixed costs of new workers tends to decrease the length. In terms of the desire to change the equilibrium value of the stock of senior workers by altering the flow into senior status, these results are understandable. The other partials are ambiguous, which again is not disturbing given the complexity of the system.

Dynamics

Eliminating λ_1 and λ_2 from (3.5a)–(3.5g), our dynamic system can be reduced to five equations in M_1, H_1, $\dot{M}_2$, and $\dot{\theta}$ (given M_2 and θ at each point in time).

$$\dot{M}_2 - \theta M_1 + q_2 M_2 = 0 \tag{3.13a}$$

$$M_1 \beta(H_1) + M_2 K \beta(H_2) - L = 0 \tag{3.13b}$$

$$\beta'(H_1) - \gamma_2 K \beta'(H_2) = 0 \tag{3.13c}$$

$$w_1 \gamma_1 + w_2(1-b)\gamma_2 \bar{H} + w_2 b \gamma_2 \left[H_1 - \frac{\beta(H_1)}{\beta'(H_1)} \right] + c(\theta) - \theta c'(0) = 0 \tag{3.13d}$$

$$c''(\theta)\dot{\theta} - (r + q_2)c'(\theta) - w_1 - w_2(1-b)\bar{H} - w_2 b \left[H_2 - \frac{\beta(H_2)}{\beta'(H_2)} \right] = 0 \tag{3.13e}$$

In order to analyze the dynamics of the model, it is first necessary to take the differential of the system, holding all parameters constant, and obtain in matrix form

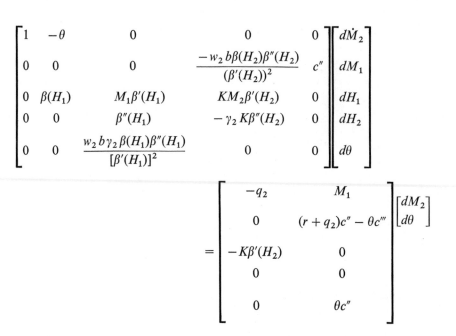

Denote the determinant of the 5 by 5 matrix on the left-hand side by E and let E_{ij} be the cofactor of the ith row and jth column of that matrix. Then tedious calculation again indicates that[19]

$$[E_{ij}] = \begin{bmatrix} - & 0 & 0 & 0 & 0 \\ 0 & 0 & 0 & 0 & - \\ - & - & 0 & 0 & 0 \\ NC & NC & NC & NC & NC \\ - & - & + & + & - \end{bmatrix} \qquad E < 0 \qquad (3.14)$$

We can now construct our dynamic analysis in (θ, M_2) space. The locus of points for which the stock of senior employees is a constant (the $\dot{M}_2 = 0$ singular curve) is given from (3.13a) by

$$\theta = q_2 \frac{M_2}{M_1} \qquad (3.15)$$

---

[19] "NC" indicates not calculated. The explicit values of E and E_{ij} are listed in the appendix to the chapter for reference, since they are used extensively in what follows.

The slope of this curve is given by,

$$\frac{\partial \theta}{\partial M_2}\bigg|_{\dot{M}_2=0} = q_2 \left[\frac{M_1 - M_2 \dfrac{\partial M_1}{\partial M_2}}{M_2^2}\right]$$

However, using Cramer's Rule,

$$\frac{\partial M_1}{\partial M_2} = -q_2 \frac{E_{12}}{E} - K\beta'(H_2) \frac{E_{32}}{E} < 0$$

Hence the $\dot{M}_2 = 0$ singular curve is positively sloped as indicated in Figure 3–1.

The locus of points for which the length of the training period is constant (the $\dot{\theta} = 0$ singular curve) is given from equation (3.13c) by

$$c'(\theta) = \frac{-bw_2}{(r+q_2)}\left[H_2 - \frac{\beta(H_2)}{\beta'(H_2)}\right] - \left[\frac{w_1 + w_2(1-b)\bar{H}}{(r+q_2)}\right] \tag{3.16}$$

Its slope is therefore,

$$\frac{\partial \theta}{\partial M_2}\bigg|_{\dot{\theta}=0} = \frac{-bw_2\,\beta(H_2)\beta'(H_2)}{(r+q_2)c''[\beta'(H_2)]^2}\frac{\partial H_2}{\partial M_2}$$

However,

$$\frac{\partial H_2}{\partial M_2} = -q_2 \frac{E_{14}}{E} - K\beta'(H_2) \frac{E_{34}}{O} = 0$$

Therefore the $\dot{\theta} = 0$ singular curve is a horizontal line, as drawn in Figure 3–1. The intersection of the two singular curves indicates the long-run stationary solution. To see if this solution will indeed be reached, we calculate the directional movement of points in the phase space. We assume here that $\dot{\theta}c'''$ is small enough to be dominated by $(r+q_2)c''$. This will be true at least in a neighborhood of equilibrium, or always if $c''' = 0$ (training costs are quadratic). Note first that

$$\frac{\partial \dot{\theta}}{\partial \theta}\bigg|_{M_2} = M_1 \frac{E_{15}}{E} + [(r+q_2)c'' - \dot{\theta}c'''] \frac{E_{25}}{E} + \theta c'' \frac{E_{55}}{E} > 0 \tag{3.17}$$

That is above (below) the $\dot{\theta} = 0$ singular curve, $\dot{\theta}$ is positive (negative) and hence θ is increasing (decreasing) as the vertical arrows indicate. Similarly

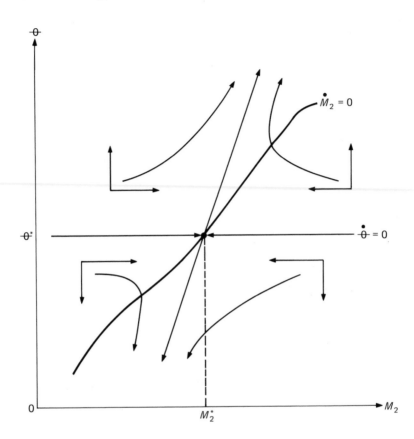

Figure 3–1.

$$\left.\frac{\partial \dot{M}_2}{\partial M_2}\right|_\theta = -q_2 \frac{E_{11}}{E} - K\beta'(H_2)\frac{E_{31}}{E} < 0 \qquad (3.18)$$

To the right (left) of the $\dot{M}_2 = 0$ singular curve, $\dot{M}_2$ is negative (positive) and thus M_2 is decreasing (increasing) as the horizontal arrows in Figure 3–1 indicate.

As the directional arrows indicate, to eventually reach a stationary equilibrium requires setting $1/\theta$, the length of the training period, immediately equal to its long-run equilibrium value and *not* varying it during the transition to equilibrium. This path satisfies the transversality condition (3.5h) and indeed it can be shown that all other paths either violate the transversality condition or the condition that θ always be positive. Hence, although the length of the training period is a decision variable in the long run, the optimality conditions require that it should not be altered in the short run. We note, in passing, that it can be shown that the integrand is appropriately concave so that the necessary conditions are also sufficient for a minimal path.[20]

Next observe that

$$\frac{\partial \dot{M}_2}{\partial M_2} = \frac{\partial \dot{M}_2}{\partial M_2}\bigg|_{\theta} + \frac{\partial \dot{M}_2}{\partial \theta}\frac{\partial \theta}{\partial M_2} \tag{3.19}$$

Since we have just shown that along the optimal path $\partial\theta/\partial M_2 = 0$, this reduces to equation (3.18). Substituting the explicit values of E, E_{11}, E_{31} from the appendix to this chapter, we find that

$$\frac{\partial \dot{M}_2}{\partial M_2} = -\left[\frac{q_2\beta(H_1) + K\beta'(H_1)\theta}{\beta(H_1)}\right] \tag{3.20}$$

That is, crucially over the relevant range we have the flow of workers into seniority status related to the existing stock of senior workers by a "stock adjustment" equation of the form

$$\dot{M}_2 = c_1(M_2^* - M_2) \tag{3.21}$$

The adjustment coefficient c_1 is equal to the expression in brackets in equation (3.20) and is *not* constant across firms since H_1 and θ are functions of all of the parameters in the model *except* desired labor services, as can be seen from equation (3.12). It is also useful to observe how the stock of new workers is related to the stock of senior workers.

$$\frac{\partial M_1}{\partial M_2} = -q_2\frac{E_{12}}{E} - K\beta'(H_2)\frac{E_{32}}{E} = -\left[\frac{K\beta'(H_2)}{\beta(H_1)}\right] \tag{3.22}$$

---

[20] See Arrow [2], proposition 5, p. 10 on this.

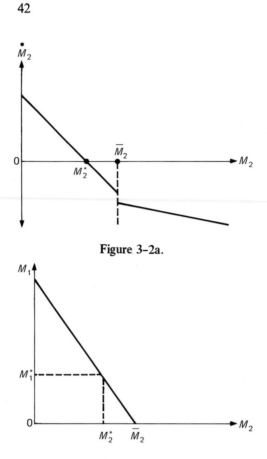

Figure 3–2a.

Figure 3–2b.

Thus, we can write[21]

$$M_1 = c_2(M_2^* - M_2) + \frac{q_2}{\theta} M_2^* \qquad (3.23)$$

---

[21] Implicitly we have assumed throughout that $M_{20} < \overline{M}_2$ as defined in Figures 3–2a and 3–2b. Otherwise we would be faced with a negative level of M_1—economically nonsensical. Alternatively, we could explicitly restrict $M_1 \geq 0$ and formulate the problem using Pontryagin techniques. For $M_1 > 0$ our results would be identical. For the boundary, $M_1 = 0$, from equation (3.13a), $M_2 = -q_2 M_2$. Hence in absolute terms the slope of the M_2 curve becomes smaller at M_2. There may also be a "jump" in the path, as indicated in Figure 3–2a, although this is not necessary.

Here c_2 is the term in brackets in equation (3.22) and is again a function of all the parameters in the model except desired labor services. The second term in equation (3.23) represents the long-run equilibrium level of M_1 while the first term represents the disequilibrium level, i.e.,

$$(M_1 - M_1^*) = c_2(M_2^* - M_2) \qquad (3.24)$$

In this model, much of the adjustment to long-run equilibrium is done by hiring and laying off new workers. Since we have assumed that this can be done at essentially zero cost, this is not surprising. Somewhat surprising, *at first glance*, are the following results though.[22]

$$\frac{\partial H_1}{\partial M_2} = -q_2 \frac{E_{13}}{E} - K\beta'(H_2)\frac{E_{33}}{E} = 0$$

$$\qquad (3.25)$$

$$\frac{\partial H_2}{\partial M_2} = -q_2 \frac{E_{14}}{E} - K\beta'(H_2)\frac{E_{34}}{E} = 0$$

We have generated a model in which hours of both classes of labor are *constant* along the dynamic adjustment path. This phenomenon requires some explanation. In our earlier homogeneous labor model, a lagged adjustment of the employment stock *technically* required, from the labor input function constraint, that hours vary along the adjustment path. In this model, the adjustment is made solely by altering the number of new hires. With the four input labor-services function (3.13b), the deviation of M_2 from its equilibrium value does not imply that either H_1 or H_2 must deviate from their equilibrium values.

The empirical observation that the average workweek varies seasonally and cyclically does not contradict the above conclusion. First, as we shall indicate in detail in the next section, even if H_1 and H_2 are constant, observed average hours per man will vary along the adjustment path as the M_1/M_2 ratio varies. Second, and perhaps more important, the assumptions of the model should be emphasized. The model assumes static expectations on the level of required labor services; ignores uncertainty and seasonal factors;

---

[22] This is strictly true only when $M_1 > 0$ (see above). If we initially have an excess of senior workers ($M_{20} > \overline{M_2}$) then $M_1 = 0$ and the motion of the system is governed by $M_2 = -q_2\overline{M_2}$, $L = M_2 K\beta(H_2)$. It is easy to see that $\partial H_2/\partial M_2 < 0$ in this region. That is, as in our earlier models, if the stock of senior workers is too large, hours per man must decrease. We have assumed, however, that we are close enough to equilibrium such that $M_1 > 0$.

and crucially assumes that an infinitely elastic supply of new workers is available at an exogeneously given wage rate, with the marginal cost of training each new worker (given θ) independent of the size of the labor stock. In periods of high demand, with low unemployment (especially among skilled workers), it is more appropriate to assume that the firm faces a positively sloped (in terms of men) supply of labor and hence might tend to substitute overtime for additional employment. Since we have abstracted from uncertainty, seasonality, and positively sloped labor supply functions here, there is no reason to expect hours of either class to vary along the adjustment path.

The Aggregation Problem

Our cross-section empirical work utilizes individual establishment data in an attempt to determine the causes of intraindustry variations in observed overtime hours per man. Customarily, the assumption is made in cross-section studies that long-run equilibrium positions of firms in the sample are being compared. However, after constructing a dynamic model, one may seek to ascertain what problems will arise if firms are not all in long-run equilibrium but are located in short-run equilibrium along the dynamic adjustment path. Since, in the present model, hours of each class of workers are constant along this path, one potential problem is eliminated. We are faced, however, with an aggregation problem, since the observed value of hours per man (H_0) is a weighted average of the unobservable variables hours per new worker (H_1) and hours per senior worker (H_2). From equation (3.24), it is obvious that the ratio of new to senior workers varies along the adjustment path. Hence even if two firms face identical parameters, if H_1 is not equal to H_2 and the two firms are at different points on the path, then observed hours per man (H_0) will vary between them. This will distort our empirical results unless we can predict how H_0 will vary.

Fortunately, with one further empirical assumption, we are able to solve the problem. We assume that the parameters γ_1, γ_2, K, and r do not vary across firms in a given industry. Then collecting the results of the previous sections, we have that

$$H_1 = H_1^*(w_1, w_2, b, \overline{H}, q) \tag{3.26a}$$

$$H_2 = H_2^* = g(\gamma_2 K)H_1^* \quad \text{where } g(\gamma_2 K) \gtreqqless 1 \quad \text{as } \gamma_2 K \gtreqqless 1 \tag{3.26b}$$

$$\theta = \theta^*(w_1, w_2, b, \overline{H}, q) \tag{3.26c}$$

$$\dot{M}_2 = c_1(M_2^* - M_2) = \dot{M}_2(w_1, w_2, b, \bar{H}, q, L, M_2) \qquad (3.26\text{d})$$

$$M_1 = c_2(M_2^* - M_2) + M_1^* = M_1(w_1, w_2, b, \bar{H}, q, L, M_2) \qquad (3.26\text{e})$$

At any point in time

$$H_0 = \frac{M_1 H_1 + M_2 H_2}{M_1 + M_2} \qquad (3.27)$$

Substituting for H_2 from equation and dividing both numerator and denominator by M_2, this can be written

$$H_0 = H_1 \left[\frac{\dfrac{M_1}{M_2} + g(\gamma_2 K)}{\dfrac{M_1}{M_2} + 1} \right]$$

Differentiating with respect to the ratio of new to senior workers, we obtain

$$\frac{\partial H_0}{\partial \left(\dfrac{M_1}{M_2}\right)} = \frac{H_1}{\left(\dfrac{M_1}{M_2} + 1\right)^2} (1 - g(\gamma_2 K)) \gtreqless 0 \quad \text{as } K \lesseqgtr \frac{1}{\gamma_2} \quad \text{or} \quad \gamma_2 K \lesseqgtr 1 \qquad (3.28)$$

Hence to account for the disequilibrium aggregation bias, the appropriate cross-section regression equation should be

$$H_0 = H_0(w_1, w_2, b, \bar{H}, q, M_1/M_2) \qquad (3.29)$$

Note that the sign of the coefficient of the ratio of new to senior workers in this regression will enable us to make statements about the average (assumed constant within industries) value of $\gamma_2 K$ for firms in each industry. From this we can determine from condition (8), those industries in which it would be rational to assign overtime on the basis of seniority.

The problem is not completely solved yet, however. At any instant of time we may take M_2 as a predetermined variable. But dividing (3.26c) by M_2, we observe that the ratio of new to senior workers is indeed an endogenous variable in the system.

$$\frac{M_1}{M_2} = \frac{M_1}{M_2} (w_1, w_2, b, \bar{H}, q, L, M_2) \qquad (3.30)$$

Thus, to appropriately account for the disequilibrium aggregation bias it is necessary to estimate equations (3.29) and (3.30) jointly using simultaneous equation methods.

One further complication still exists with regard to the interpretation of the estimated regression coefficients of equation (3.29). When a parameter changes, it effects observed hours in two ways. First it changes the equilibrium values of H_1^* and H_2^*. Second, and unfortunately, it alters the ratio of new to senior workers. Hence, even if changing a parameter causes both H_1^* and H_2^* to increase, H_0 may actually decrease since the weights used in computing it have changed.

More precisely, when firms are spaced along the dynamic adjustment path, we know from equations (3.22), (3.23), and (3.27) that

$$H_0 = H_1^* \frac{\left[\dfrac{M_1}{M_2} + g(\gamma_2 K)\right]}{\left(\dfrac{M_1}{M_2} + 1\right)} \tag{3.31a}$$

$$\frac{M_1}{M_2} = \frac{K\beta'(H_2^*)}{\beta(H_1^*)}\left(\frac{M_2^*}{M_2} - 1\right) + \frac{M_1^*}{M_2} \tag{3.31b}$$

Differentiating, remembering that at an instant of time we may take M_2 as predetermined, we have that for $x = w_1, w_2, \bar{H}, b, q_2$

$$\frac{\partial H_0}{\partial x}\left[\frac{\dfrac{M_1}{M_2} + g(\gamma_2 K)}{\dfrac{M_1}{M_2} + 1}\right]\frac{\partial H_1^*}{\partial x} + \left[\frac{H_1^*}{\left(\dfrac{M_1}{M_2} + 1\right)^2}\right][1 - g(\gamma_2 K)]\frac{\partial\left(\dfrac{M_1}{M_2}\right)}{\partial x} \tag{3.32a}$$

where

$$\frac{\partial\left(\dfrac{M_1}{M_2}\right)}{\partial x} = \left[\frac{K\beta'(H_2^*)}{\beta(H_1^*)M_2}\right]\frac{\partial M_2^*}{\partial x} + \frac{1}{M_2}\frac{\partial M_1^*}{\partial x}$$

$$+ \left(\frac{M_2^*}{M_2} - 1\right)\left(\frac{K}{(\beta(H_1^*))^2}\right)\left[\beta(H_1^*)\beta''(H_2^*)\frac{\partial H_2^*}{\partial x} - \beta'(H_1^*)\beta'(H_2^*)\frac{\partial H_1^*}{\partial x}\right] \tag{3.32b}$$

Since a change in any parameter effects M_1^* and M_2^* as well as H_1^* and H_2^*, we find that the partials of H_0 and H_1 (or H_2) need not be of the same signs. Sufficient but not necessary conditions for the signs to be the same are either $\gamma_2 K$ close to unity or that the net effect of the three terms in equation (3.32b) is to make the ratio of new to senior workers "unresponsive" to parameter changes.

Equations (3.32a) and (3.32b) indicate that extreme care must be taken in interpreting estimated regression equations. For even if the signs of the partials of observed and true hours are the same, their magnitudes may differ greatly. It is the quantitative estimate of the true partials which are important for policy purposes and any conclusions that are drawn should keep this fact in mind.

Conclusion

In this chapter we have attempted to build a dynamic model of firm behavior which incorporated certain aspects of the "internal labor market." Through our assumptions of a seniority structure, productivity and wage differentials, and on-the-job training, we have generated answers to a variety of interesting questions: Why do different employees of a given firm work different numbers of hours? Is it rational to assign overtime on the basis of seniority? Will the fact that all firms are not in long-run equilibrium effect our cross-section results? Can we solve the "aggregation problem" caused by the heterogeneity of labor? These questions are all satisfactorily answered for the specific model presented here.

Heterogeneity of labor, and the introduction of the length of the training period as a decision variable, led us to some results that are contrary to one's *initial* economic intuition. Several of the comparative static results concerning the long-run equilibrium stocks were ambiguous and we have attempted to explain why. Also, we found that hours per man for both classes are constant along the adjustment path and we sought to explain the plausibility of this result. The combination of previous exposure to models with homogeneous labor, and empirical observation of aggregated variables from an uncertain world, may have indeed colored our vision. That is, in a certainty world with low costs of hiring and laying off new workers, why should hours rather than new hires adjust? The homogeneous labor model predicts that hours will adjust due to the *technical* constraint that if the employment stock is less than optimal, then hours must be greater than optimal in order to satisfy the fixed labor-services requirement. This argument is independent of any economic content and once we move to the heterogeneous labor case, it fails to be valid.

The model has greater application to other labor market problems than might be obvious in this chapter. We have noted that in a partial equilibrium context, a decrease in the relative wage of unskilled labor need not necessarily increase their employment, contrary to the views widely expressed. In fact, one obvious extension is to make the relative wage (γ_2) a decision variable in the model by letting the senior workers' quit rate (q_2) be an endogeneous variable which is a function of the relative wage. Given the institutional framework of our model, we may be able to generate explanations for why the "skill differential"[23] varies across industries, or has varied historically in a given industry. Other possible extensions include increasing the number of classes of workers in the hope of more explicitly building learning into the model and to separate the length of the training period from the period necessary to achieve seniority. Since neither of these extensions is directly relevant to the empirical problem at hand, they will not be undertaken here.

---

[23] This is Reder's [57] terminology. In the context of our model we are still referring to γ_2.

4
The Data: Some Problems of Classification and Measurement

The data utilized in the empirical sections of the study are derived from unpublished individual establishment data released to us from the Bureau of Labor Statistics' survey of " Employer Expenditures for Selected Compensation Practices, 1966."[1] This survey encompassed the entire U.S. private nonagricultural sector and contained information on employer compensation expenditures actually made during the period January 1 to December 31, 1966. While the survey included data for both office and related workers and nonoffice workers, only the latter category of employees were considered in our study.[2] Many employees in the former category are exempt from the overtime provisions of the Fair Labor Standards Act [87] and indeed are not even paid on an hourly basis. Consequently, we would not expect our theoretical models to explain the overtime behavior of this group.

Establishments were selected for inclusion in the sample on a probability basis, with the probability of inclusion being proportionate to the number of workers employed. All establishments with greater than 10,000 employees were included, while other establishments were included with a probability equal to the establishment's employment divided by 12,000.[3] A sample of 4,009 establishments employing 6.326 million workers was eventually obtained, as compared to the universe of 1,807,094 establishments and 53.111 million workers in the 1966 private nonagricultural economy. The sample that we received was reduced to 3,665 establishments, as any large establishment that could be easily identified was eliminated to avoid violating the confidentiality pledge made while collecting the raw data. Many of the eliminated " establishment records " in fact contained information from company-wide reports, covering more than one establishment. Since our theories implicitly assumed a single-location firm, the elimination of these observations is actually desirable.

---

[1] I am indebted to Commissioner Thomas Gavett of the B.L.S. and the members of his staff for making this data available to me. The data were made unidentifiable by the elimination of the name and location of each establishment before being released to me.

[2] These categories correspond to those of nonproduction and production workers respectively in the manufacturing, mining, and construction industries.

[3] Only establishments with greater than four employees were considered for inclusion.

Data similar to those underlying this study has been collected by the B.L.S. in 1959, 1962, and 1968 for the manufacturing industries. Although aggregated information based on the 1959 and 1962 surveys has been published [78], [79], the underlying individual establishment data is no longer accessible for those years. The 1968 survey data is currently being processed and may be available for researchers' use in the future. Because of these facts, the present study was restricted to the single year, 1966. Consideration of such problems as ascertaining the stability of estimated regression coefficients over time, consequently had to be postponed until a later date.

The remainder of this chapter considers two problems of classification and measurement. First, which supplementary compensation practices can be legitimately thought of as being "quasi-fixed," in the sense of not varying as overtime hours per man vary? Secondly, does the observed variable overtime hours per man correspond to our theoretical construct, and if not, what problems will arise in our empirical work? The appendix to this chapter contains a description of the data and explicitly indicates how each of the variables used in our empirical work was calculated. For several of these variables, more than one empirical "definition" was possible, and an explanation for why a particular "definition" was chosen for inclusion in the *reported* empirical work is also found there.

Classification of the Supplementary Compensation Expenditures[4]

In this section, we briefly consider the problem of classifying the various supplementary compensation categories for which we have data, as either quasi-fixed or man-hour related. The distinction is crucially based on how the employer finances an expenditure, not on how the benefits from an expenditure are allocated. For example, if an employer "purchases" health insurance for each of his employees by contributing five cents per man-hour

---

[4] This section draws heavily on the following sources: Bureau of Labor Statistics publications such as [81], [82], [83], [85], [86], Bureau of Employment Security Publications [74], [75], [76], J. Becker [7], B. Hughes [36] and Chamber of Commerce Publications [13]. Since the method of financing the various fringes varies widely across establishments, the statements in the text should be interpreted as indicating general impressions gotten from the above sources. The discussion is necessarily brief and superficial here; an adequate discussion of the topic would take volumes. For example, Becker [7] has devoted a book solely to the workings of the various supplementary unemployment compensation benefit plans and in a yet unfinished Princeton dissertation B. Hughes [36] studies the compensation structure of the automobile industry in detail. Our discussion is intended only to indicate which items might reasonably be considered quasi-fixed for the majority of establishments in our sample.

worked into a union welfare fund, then the cost is man-hour related even though benefits accrue on a per man basis. The supplementary compensation expenditures contained in the survey can be conveniently grouped into the four categories found in Table 4–1; each category will be discussed below.

Table 4–1. Supplementary Compensation Expenditures Contained in the B.L.S. Survey

A. *Legally Required Insurance*
  1. Unemployment compensation
  2. Social Security (OASDI)
  3. Workmen's Compensation and other legally required

B. *Payments Directly to Employees as Part of Payroll*
  1. Vacation payments
  2. Holiday payments
  3. Civic and sick leave
  4. Nonproduction bonuses
  5. Terminal payments

C. *Private Welfare Plans*
  1. Life insurance
  2. Health insurance
  3. Pension and retirement plans

D. *Payment to Funds*
  1. Vacation and holiday funds
  2. Savings and thrift plans
  3. Severence and SUB funds
  4. Other private welfare plans

Source: See appendix to this chapter.

Legally Required Insurance

Both federal and state unemployment compensation taxes are payroll taxes with annual earnings per employee taxed at a flat rate until earnings exceed the maximum taxable wage base. In 1966, the taxable wage base was $3,000 per employee in 28 of the 50 states, with only four states having bases greater than $4,000 per employee.[5] For those employees whose annual earnings exceeded the maximum taxable level, the unemployment compensation costs do not vary with additional overtime hours. The tax rate varies across industries and states, with almost all states determining the appropriate tax rate for a firm by its "experience rating."[6] That is, establishments with high turnover tend to pay

---

[5] See [73].

[6] In 1964, the national average tax rate was 2.2 percent, not a negligible figure. See [74].

higher tax rates. This provides a further incentive to substitute overtime for additional employment.

Employer social security (OASDI) contributions are also financed by a payroll tax, but the tax base is a good deal higher than that for unemployment compensation insurance. In 1966, contributions were required on annual earnings per man up to the level of $6,000 and this tax base has been steadily increasing since then. Average annual earnings per man within almost all two-digit industries, as calculated for establishments in our sample, did not exceed this figure in 1966. Consequently, employer social security contributions had to be made for overtime hours and it is probably *not* appropriate to consider social security payment as quasi-fixed costs.[7]

Workmen's compensation and other legally required insurance programs vary in nature across states and industries. No information is available to us concerning the financing of those programs; indeed the data do not even tell us which programs are included in the latter category. We therefore somewhat arbitrarily classify these programs as being "man" related. Given the magnitude of these costs, especially for the latter category, this classification should not result in a serious measurement error.

Payments Directly to Employees as Part of Payroll

Paid vacations are usually a specified number of weeks per employee each year with vacation pay based on straight-time weekly earnings, in which cases these costs are quasi-fixed.[8] In some cases, however, vacation pay received is a percentage of the employee's total annual earnings including overtime pay. Our impression is that the latter method is not prevalent. As noted in the previous chapter, the number of weeks vacation a year to which an employee is entitled, often varies with seniority. This fact has been accounted for in our theoretical model.

The number of paid holidays that a full-time employee receives is generally independent of the amount of overtime that he works, although it may again be based to a degree on his seniority. Paid sick leave is similarly

---

[7] This generalization may be incorrect. Suppose, as before, that there are two classes of workers in each establishment. The observed establishment mean annual income per man may be less than $6,600, but if it is the "senior" employees who work the overtime and their incomes exceed $6,600, then additional overtime worked by them does not increase employer social security contributions.

[8] See the various B.L.S. *Wage Chronologies* [81].

structured; each employee is usually entitled to a specified number of days or hours per year. Leave for civic obligations is also independent of hours of work.[9]

The last two items in this category, nonproduction bonuses and terminal payments, include only payments made directly to employees; not those made to union–management welfare funds. Lump-sum severance pay is usually based only on years of service and nonproduction bonuses such as lump-sum Christmas bonuses to employees seem to be independent of overtime hours.[10] In sum, it appears that all of the items in category B of Table 4–1 can legitimately be considered as quasi-fixed costs.

Private Welfare Plans

Employers often contribute at least a portion of the premium payments for employees' group life and health insurance plans. As might be expected, in most establishments where the employer finances his obligation directly, as opposed to contributing to a union welfare fund, his costs are on a per man basis and independent of hours of work.[11] Again, however, it is important to realize that periods of employment are often required before the employee becomes eligible for these benefits, and during such periods the employer has no contributions to make.

The financing of pension and retirement plans is exceedingly complicated. What is crucial is how the employer finances the obligations, not how eligibility for benefits is determined. Methods of financing vary widely, but in the majority of cases employer liabilities appear to be related to expected outlays to be made from the fund. Flat-benefit plans providing a fixed monthly pension which is a function of years of service, appear to be fairly common, especially among multiemployer and union plans.[12] Since these benefits do not vary with overtime hours, it is likely that the employers' obligations do not either.[13]

---

[9] Civic leave includes leave for categories such as military obligations, jury duty, and time off to vote in elections.

[10] See the various B.L.S. *Wage Chronologies* [81].

[11] See [82].

[12] See B.L.S. *Wage Chronologies* [81].

[13] A year of service is often defined in terms of a minimum required number of hours worked during the year. This number can usually be achieved by a full-time employee without his working any overtime, unless he is laid off during the course of the year.

Payments to Funds

In several industries, vacation and holiday pay for employees are financed by employers making contributions to union welfare funds, with the union then administering the benefits to its members. Even if these benefits are "man-related," if the employer finances them on a per man-hour basis, they should not be considered as quasi-fixed costs.[14] It appears that many of these funds as well as the "Saving and Thrift Plans" and the category of expenditures "Other Private Welfare Plans" are financed this way. Similarly, most severance pay and supplementary unemployment compensation plans are financed on a per man-hour basis.[15] Consequently, the bulk of the category "Payments to Funds" probably should be excluded from the quasi-fixed costs.

As we indicate in the appendix to this chapter, two separate variables representing the weekly quasi-fixed costs per man were actually calculated. The first variable included all of the expenditure items found in Table 4–1, while the second excluded social security payments and the items in the category "Payments to Funds." Across establishments within a given two-digit industry, the correlation between the two measures was always greater than 0.97. Not surprisingly, therefore, regression results using the two measures were only marginally different. Consequently, we report in the next two chapters the results only for the regressions in which the first variable was used.

This should not be interpreted as implying that results using this variable were always "better" in some statistical sense than results using the alternative, perhaps more theoretically justifiable, variable. Indeed this was not the case. Rather, this variable was chosen because its use enables us to directly calculate from the estimated regression coefficients, what the effect on the level of overtime hours per man would be if the overtime premium were increased.[16]

In concluding this section it is relevant to indicate that the B.L.S. survey does not contain information about several types of labor costs which might be considered as quasi-fixed. These costs include items such as travel-time allowances; compensation for clothing, uniforms, and equipment; paid

---

[14] I.e., if he contributes ten cents per man-hour to the union welfare fund.

[15] See J. Becker [7].

[16] This is done in Chapter 7. Use of the other variable would mean that increasing the overtime premium by say 50 percent would increase the hourly cost of overtime by less than 50 per cent, since no overtime premium is paid on hourly-related fringe costs. The exact percentage increases in hourly costs might vary across establishments and thus the effect on the level of overtime in each establishment would be more difficult to calculate.

lunch and rest periods; clothes' changing time; educational allowances; and part of the costs of the personnel department. In addition, no data on the hiring and training costs of new employees is available. Consequently, our measure of the ratio of weekly "fixed costs" to the overtime wage rate (*RATIO*) is probably biased downward for all establishments in the sample. If within a two-digit industry the "true" fixed costs are a constant ($c > 1$) multiple of the observed fixed costs, then the estimated regression coefficient of *RATIO* will be biased upwards by this multiple. Since the upward bias in the regression coefficient exactly cancels out the downward bias in the numerator of the *RATIO* variable, the estimated net effect of the *RATIO* variable on overtime will be unbiased. Moreover, we can directly calculate, as mentioned above, an unbiased estimate of the effect of an increase in the overtime premium on overtime hours per man.

The Measurement of Overtime

The concept of overtime implicit in our theoretical models is straightforward: After a specified number of hours of work per week (or day), an employee receives a premium wage rate for any additional hours that he works. These additional hours are considered overtime hours. For example, in industries covered by the Fair Labor Standards Act, covered employees must receive at least "time-and-a-half" for all hours over forty which they work a week.

Unfortunately, our observed overtime variable does not conform to this theoretical construct. Observed overtime includes all hours for which premium pay is received.[17] Union rules often require that "overtime pay" be received for all hours worked during weekends, paid holidays, paid vacations, or the six and seventh work day of a week, regardless of the number of hours previously worked by an employee during the week.[18] Union rules may also require that employees be guaranteed specified amounts of overtime. We attempt to account for these factors by including a zero-one dummy variable, which indicates if the majority of the establishments' employees are covered by collective bargaining agreements, as an explanatory variable in most of the regressions estimated in subsequent chapters. If unions affect the level of overtime, rather than just altering the periods when it is worked, we would expect this variable to have a positive coefficient.

A potentially more serious problem exists, in that both the static and dynamic models presented previously, explain only variations in *equilibrium*

---

[17] Excluding only shift premiums.

[18] See various B.L.S. *Wage Chronologies* [81].

levels of overtime. There is no doubt, however, that the bulk of overtime hours that are worked are due to *disequilibrium* factors such as emergencies, rush orders, and uncertainty about the permanence of increases in demand. These factors are not considered in our theoretical models. At least three possible ways of handling this problem econometrically appear to exist:

Since observed overtime per man will always be greater than the equilibrium level of overtime which our models predict, one way of handling the problem is to use constrained regression analysis and minimize the sum of squared residuals (or the sum of the absolute values of the residuals) subject to the constraint that predicted overtime be less than observed overtime for each observation. That is, choose a vector of coefficients $\hat{\beta}$ to

$$\text{minimize} \quad \sum_{i=1}^{n}(y_i - \hat{y}_i)^2 = \sum_{i=1}^{n}(y_i - x_i'\hat{\beta})^2 \qquad (14.1)$$

$$\text{subject to} \quad \hat{y}_i \leq y_i \quad \text{for} \quad i = 1, \ldots, n$$

Here y_i is the observed value of overtime per man for the ith establishment, $\hat{y}_i$ is the estimated value of overtime per man to be determined by the model, x_i is a vector of explanatory variables for "equilibrium" overtime for the ith establishment, and n is the number of establishments in the sample. This type of estimation technique was initially suggested by Charnes, Cooper, and Ferguson [15]; Fisher [27]; and Wagner [89], among others. It has been recently applied to the estimation of production functions by Aigner and Chu [1].

Under certain nonrestrictive assumptions, Charnes, Cooper and Ferguson [15] showed that coefficient estimates obtained via such methods will be consistent, however, little else is known about the statistical properties of these estimators.[19] This method is also computationally tedious and it is not clear how it could be extended to handle the simultaneity problem discussed in Chapter 3. Consequently, it appeared wise not to adopt this approach in our study.

A related way of attacking the problem is to assume that there is a measurement error in the dependent variable (equilibrium overtime hours per man). That is, we postulate a true relationship of the form

$$y_i^* = (x_i^*)'\beta + \varepsilon_i \qquad \varepsilon \sim n(0, \nabla^2 I) \qquad (4.2)$$

y^* is now equilibrium overtime hours per man, x^* is again the vector of

---

[19] Some work has been done in this area, including Monte Carlo studies. See Zellner [91] and Ashar and Wallace [3].

explanatory variables derived from our theoretical models (including a constant term), and ε an error term that satisfies all the Gauss–Markov assumptions. Observed overtime hours per man (y) is always greater than equilibrium overtime per man, therefore

$$y_i = y_i^* + u_i \qquad (4.3)$$

where $E(u) \geq 0$, $u \geq 0$, and we assume u and ε are uncorrelated.

Substituting equation (4.3) into equation (4.2) and adding and subtracting the expected value of the measurement error yields

$$y_i = E(u) + (x_i^*)'\beta + v_i \quad \text{where} \quad v_i = \varepsilon_i + u_i - E(u) \qquad E(v) = 0 \quad (4.4)$$

That is, the measurement error in the dependent variable is absorbed into the constant term. If u and x^* are uncorrelated, since all the other classical assumptions hold, the ordinary least squares estimate of β will be unbiased except for the intercept term which will be biased upwards. Note, however, that v cannot be normally distributed because u is restricted to be nonnegative. Consequently, if this approach is adopted, conventional significance tests on coefficients and other tests of hypotheses cannot legitimately be made.

The approach actually adopted does not emphasize measurement errors in the dependent variable. Rather, we treat the problem as a problem in omitted explanatory variables. Observed overtime hours per man (y) can be divided into two components, its equilibrium component (y^*) which is "explained" by the vector of explanatory variables derived from our models (x^*), and its disequilibrium component (y^d) which is "explained" by a set of unobservable variables (x^d). This set might include variables such as whether a machine broke down on a particular day, the number of rush orders, etc. Suppose that the true relationship is

$$y_i = y_i^* + y_i^d = (x_i^*)'\beta + (x_i^d)'\gamma + \varepsilon_i \qquad \varepsilon \sim n(0, \nabla^2 I) \qquad (4.5)$$

Here β and γ are the vector of regression coefficients associated with x^* and x^d respectively. For each establishment, we can observe only y and x^*. However, a well-known theorem states that if the omitted variables (x^d) are uncorrelated with any of the remaining explanatory variables (x^*), then regressing the dependent variable (y) on the remaining explanatory variables (x^*) will yield an unbiased estimate of their coefficients (β).[20] Our work in the following chapters essentially makes this zero-correlation assumption, although in several places the assumption is modified.

---

[20] See Theil [68] or Malinvaud [46] for example.

5

Overtime Behavior in U.S. Manufacturing Industries, 1966

This chapter presents the results of an empirical analysis of intraindustry variations in overtime behavior in the U.S. manufacturing industries in 1966. The theoretical models and discussion contained in the previous chapters suggested that the following relationship be estimated empirically,

$$OT = F(w_1/w_2 b, \bar{H}, q, M_1/M_2, 1 - a, c\beta) \qquad (5.1)$$

where $F_1 > 0$, $F_2 < 0$, $F_3 > 0$, $F_6 > 0$, and $F_4, F_5, \gtrless 0$.

The variables are defined here as previously: OT is observed annual overtime per man, $w_1/w_2 b$ is the ratio of weekly fixed costs per man to the overtime wage rate, $\bar{H}$ is the number of hours per week after which an overtime premium must be paid, q is the establishment quit rate, M_1/M_2 is the ratio of "new" to "senior" employees, $1 - a$ is the absentee rate, and $c\beta$ is a collective bargaining dummy variable.

The first explanatory variable in equation (5.1) is entered in ratio form since it can be shown theoretically that it is the ratio, rather than the levels of w_1 and $w_2 b$ independently, that influences the overtime decision. In addition this enables us to avoid a collinearity problem, because, empirically. establishments with high wage rates also tend to have high fixed labor costs. While we have direct observations for this variable, it is necessary for us to construct proxies for the other variables from the data. Given the available data, the following modification of equation (5.1) may be used as the basic estimating equation

$$OT = F(RATIO, STD.HRS, WAGE, NEWSEN, ABSEN, UNION) \quad (5.1a)$$

where $F_1 > 0$, $F_2 < 0$, $F_3 < 0$, $F_4 \gtrless 0$, $F_5 \gtrless 0$, and $F_6 > 0$.

The method of calculating these variables is discussed in detail in the appendix to Chapter 4. *RATIO* is defined as the ratio of weekly fixed costs per man to the overtime wage rate and is calculated by including *all* nonwage labor costs (for which data is available) in the numerator. A more theoretically appropriate measure that included in the denominator rather than the numerator, those "fringe" costs that vary directly with hours worked, was also calculated. The correlation between the two measures was exceedingly high in all manufacturing industries (at least 0.97) and regression results utilizing the alternative variables differed only marginally. Using the *RATIO* variable enables us to calculate directly from the estimated regression coefficients, the effect of an increase in the overtime premium on overtime hours per man. Consequently, only the regressions using this variable are reported here. The theory crucially predicts, of course, that the coefficient of this variable should be positive; an increase in the variable leads to a substitution of overtime for additional employment.

STD.HRS is a dummy variable which takes on a value of 1 if the " scheduled weekly hours " were greater than or equal to 40 and 0 otherwise. The rationale used is that those establishments that schedule their employees to work less than 40 hours probably have union contracts that require overtime premiums for some hours of work under 40. Due to the Fair Labor Standards Act [87] which almost uniformly covers manufacturing production workers, an overtime premium must be paid after 40 hours a week. Therefore, for those establishments that scheduled employees to work more than 40 hours, it was assumed that some overtime was necessarily included in the measure and that the relevant figure was 40 hours. This is an admittedly rough calculation, but it is the best that the data permits. The theory predicts that this variable be negatively related to overtime.

Turnover data is not available from the survey and hence a proxy variable must be constructed for the quit rate. The assumption here is that the higher the establishment's mean wage relative to that of other establishments in the industry, the lower its quit rate is likely to be. An alternative and perhaps more appropriate assumption is that the quit rate is negatively related to the annual earnings per employee relative to the annual earnings of employees in other establishments in the industry. Since the theory predicts a positive relationship between the quit rate and overtime, we would expect a negative relationship between overtime and either of these variables. However, empirically high relative annual earnings were highly positively correlated within an industry with overtime per man. That is, high overtime may be responsible for high annual earnings. It would, therefore, be inappropriate to use annual earnings as an independent variable and hence the relative wage rate of the establishment was used as the proxy for the quit rate.

As a proxy for the absentee rate we use *ABSEN*, the ratio of paid sick leave hours to total hours worked. We are essentially assuming that within an industry, absenteeism is a *constant* multiple of the amount of paid sick leave that is available. This may be thought of as a " Say's law of absenteeism," that the supply of paid sick leave essentially creates its own demand. The expected relationship between this variable and overtime per man is ambiguous. We have shown that an increase in a certainty absentee rate would tend to increase overtime. On the other hand, under certain conditions, a stochastic absentee rate will lead to less observed overtime than the certainty equivalent. If the "variability" of the absentee rates is not constant across firms, it is conceivable that the expected positive relationship between absenteeism and overtime per man will be obscured.

The ratio of "new" to "senior" workers is included in the estimating equation in order to account for the dynamic aggregation problem discussed in previous chapters. As a proxy for this variable we use *NEWSEN* the ratio of those employees who receive less than one week paid vacation a year to those who receive one week or more. Although paid vacations vary with seniority in most industries, the one-week dividing line is arbitrary and justified only by computational simplicity. A more complete analysis would involve a comprehensive study of union contracts and a different definition of this variable for each industry. Again the sign of the coefficient of this variable will indicate whether it is optimal to assign overtime on the basis of seniority. In particular, a negative coefficient would indicate that senior employees work longer hours than new employees, while a positive coefficient would indicate the reverse.

The final variable, *UNION*, is a dummy variable that takes on the value of unity if the majority of the firm's employees are covered by collective bargaining agreements and is zero otherwise. This variable is designed to capture the effect of union rules which require overtime pay for Saturday, Sunday, or holiday work. As will be indicated later in the chapter, this in no way captures the total effect of unions on the overtime decision. A positive coefficient for this variable would indicate that unions tend to increase the level of overtime per man.

Having completed the specification of the basic empirical model and variables to be used in the analysis, the remainder of this chapter presents the results of the empirical analysis of intraindustry variations in overtime behavior in U.S. manufacturing industries in 1966. The first section presents the results of estimating the basic equation (5.1a) while succeeding sections enlarge the analysis to consider the problem of omitted variables, simultaneous equation bias, and structural differences in the estimated relationship within a two-digit industry between (1) different size classes of firms, (2) unionized and nonunionized firms, and (3) firms in different component three-digit industries. A brief summary of the results concludes the chapter, while the discussion of implications for manpower policy is postponed until after the nonmanufacturing data are analyzed.

The Basic Linear Model

For the 16 two-digit manufacturing industries for which sufficient data (at least 20 observations) is available to conduct the analysis, equation (5.1a) was estimated in linear form.[1] Linear rather than log-linear regressions were used since observed overtime per man is a weighted average of the number of overtime hours worked by the members of each class of employees; that is, the aggregation argument refers to levels, not logarithms. In any case, although not reported here, preliminary log-linear regressions were also run and the results did not differ significantly from the linear results reported below in Table 5–1.

The most striking conclusion to be drawn from this table is that the coefficient of the *RATIO* variable is positive in all 16 manufacturing industries and significant at at least the 95 percent level in 12. Of the four industries in which it is not significant, two (Lumber S.I.C. 24 and Furniture S.I.C. 25) had relatively few observations. The Transportation industry (S.I.C. 37) is dominated by automobile manufacturing which is well known for its seasonal patterns of overtime among heterogeneous groups (production workers during production periods; retooling and maintenance workers during model changes, etc.). As such we might not expect the model to work well in this industry. Finally the Stone, Clay, and Glass industry (S.I.C. 32) is a diverse conglomeration of both continuous-process and seasonal industries. We would expect, and later tests bear us out, that it is erroneous to lump all the component three-digit industries into one two-digit industry for the purpose at hand. Thus, in spite of these four industries, the general conclusion must be one of confirming the role of fringe benefits in influencing the overtime–employment trade-off.

The coefficient of the *NEWSEN* variable was statistically significantly different from zero at at least the 90 percent level in only four of the industries. Moreover, in only one of these industries (Apparel, S.I.C. 23) was the coefficient negative, indicating that senior employees work longer hours than new employees. The failure of this coefficient to be significantly different from zero in the remaining industries is not disturbing for two reasons. First, a coefficient close to zero indicates that the relative productivity advantage of senior workers (K) is approximately equal to their relative cost disadvantage $(1/\gamma_2)$. We might expect internal wage structures to evolve this way over time.[2] Second, as we indicated in Chapter 3, since the ratio of new to senior

---

[1] The five industries for which sufficient data was not available were Ordinance and Accessories (S.I.C. 19), Tobacco (S.I.C. 21), Petroleum (S.I.C. 29), Leather (S.I.C. 31), and Instruments (S.I.C. 38). From a policy point of view, these industries were fortunately habitually among the seven manufacturing industries with the least overtime over the 1956–1966 period. In fact, in 1966, they accounted for less than 5 percent of the aggregate weekly overtime hours worked in manufacturing. See [71], p. A17.

[2] Professor Bent Hansen of Berkeley supports this viewpoint. He would argue that employers would adjust the "quality" of each class of workers over time until the relative marginal productivities would equal the relative marginal costs. This argument is outside the context of our short-run model in which the "quality" of both classes is fixed and consequently the above equality brought about entirely through variations in hours of work. That is, K is fixed rather than a choice variable in our model.

workers is itself an endogeneous variable which is a function of *RATIO*, the estimated coefficient of the *RATIO* variable will give an inaccurate impression of the effect of a change in the variable on overtime unless the coefficient of *NEWSEN* is small.[3]

ABSEN, the proxy variable for the absentee rate, has a negative coefficient in ten of the sixteen industries, although the coefficient is statistically significant in only one case. This may indicate either that the variable is a poor proxy, or that the stochastic nature of the absentee rate is confounding things. That is, if the "variability" of the absentee rate increases as the observed values of *ABSEN* increase, the observed negative relationship between *ABSEN* and overtime per man might result.

The coefficient of *WAGE* is negative as expected in almost all cases but statistically significant in only three industries. *STD.HRS* proves to be a poor proxy; its coefficient is in the main insignificantly different from zero in the intraindustry regressions, although it is negative as expected in the one case that it is significant. Finally, the *UNION* variable is significant in four industries. However, in three of the four (Textiles, Apparel, and Electric Equipment) its coefficient is negative, and in only one (Chemicals) is its coefficient positive. The implication may be that in some industries unions are seeking to limit overtime as a means of reducing unemployment among their members.

Inspection of the results in Table 5–1 indicates that many of the coefficients, especially the *RATIO* coefficients, appear to be of the same order of magnitude across industries. One may question then whether the disaggregation of the manufacturing data into industry groupings was necessary. An overall regression using all 1,003 observations from the manufacturing data was run and the results are listed in the bottom row of Table 5–1.[4] The coefficients of *RATIO* and *STD.HRS* are positive and statistically significant while those of *ABSEN* and *UNION* are negative and significant. Other than the result for *STD.HRS* these results were expected from the individual industry regressions. The positive coefficient of the *STD.HRS* variable may reflect only systematic differences in the "disequilibrium" levels of overtime across

---

[3] Or, alternatively, unless $\partial NEWSEN/\partial RATIO \approx 0$. Empirically our later two-stage least square's results indicate that this is not always the case.

[4] The assumptions needed to justify such a regression are actually extremely strong. For to assume that the structure is invariant across industries requires that
  (a) the relative wage that influences the quit rate is the one wage relative to the overall mean wage;
  (b) the technical structure of production is similar across industries;
  (c) $\gamma_2 K$ is constant across industries;
  (d) all unions behave similarly; and
  (e) disequilibrium causes of overtime (i.e., emergency rush orders) are uniform across industries.

Table 5–1. Basic Model: Ordinary Least Square (OLS) Estimates (t ratios in parentheses)

$$OT = \alpha_0 + \alpha_1 RATIO + \alpha_2 STD.HRS + \alpha_3 WAGE + \alpha_4 NEWSEN + \alpha_5 ABSEN + \alpha_6 UNION$$

Industry Number	Number of Observations	RATIO	STD.HRS	WAGE	NEWSEN	ABSEN	UNION	Constant	R^2	F
20	77	26.398[b] (2.299)	16.241 (0.099)	-51.579[a] (-1.688)	0.079 (0.083)	-3127.400 (-1.041)	-32.564 (-0.754)	179.680 (1.096)	0.134	1.816
22	137	29.898[c] (3.317)	128.920 (1.512)	-57.444 (-1.013)	0.046 (0.528)	-6566.200[a] (-1.834)	-39.371[a] (-1.699)	69.366 (0.505)	0.112	2.727
23	126	5.137[c] (3.723)	-28.108[b] (-2.109)	7.738 (0.795)	-0.041[b] (-2.340)	-2028.100 (-0.589)	-35.249[c] (-2.639)	80.023[c] (3.255)	0.204	5.090
24	25	9.876 (0.441)		-36.960 (-0.742)	0.004 (0.541)	-7120.400 (-0.972)	-106.120 (-1.379)	283.310[b] (2.271)	0.276	1.452
25	23	21.930 (0.883)	-58.731 (0.424)	-57.340 (-1.142)	-0.100 (-0.629)	-7393.500 (-1.231)	-40.262 (-0.536)	264.980 (1.260)	0.256	0.918
26	33	85.758[c] (2.763)	131.240 (0.658)	-33.610 (-0.538)	79.423 (0.808)	-2584.900 (-0.222)	87.914 (1.007)	-306.290 (-0.878)	0.256	1.487
27	35	25.793[a] (1.679)	-22.025 (-0.441)	-21.897 (-0.896)	142.210[b] (2.568)	1737.100 (0.557)	39.847 (0.701)	46.088 (0.449)	0.254	1.588
28	38	25.805[c] (2.078)		-96.996 (-0.264)	0.215 (1.463)	989.360 (0.366)	126.520[b] (2.375)	-43.149 (-0.335)	0.232	1.938
30	24	40.429[c] (2.953)		20.397 (0.449)	0.113 (0.933)	2802.800 (0.616)	-17.544 (-0.313)	-48.255 (-0.498)	0.505	3.674

Table 5-1—_Continued_

32	108	11.029 (1.091)	−39.457 (−0.271)	−80.680[b] (−0.264)	−0.081 (0.823)	6937.400 (0.512)	19.542 (0.341)	378.190[b] (2.189)	0.053	0.947
33	77	19.729[b] (2.121)		−61.798[a] (−1.656)	0.226[a] (1.710)	1673.300 (0.370)	−34.134 (−0.786)	327.940[c] (3.461)	0.110	1.746
34	92	26.392[b] (2.489)	127.190 (1.090)	−53.510 (−1.635)	0.065 (0.581)	−3139.300 (0.218)	−8.440 (−0.217)	212.920 (2.385)	0.101	1.936
35	79	33.695[c] (3.784)		−40.388 (−1.262)	−2.563 (−0.820)	2882.500 (−0.843)	−15.809 (−0.397)	83.480 (0.538)	0.222	3.428
36	66	32.481[c] (3.653)	−36.395 (−0.538)	4.573 (0.225)	4.302 (0.521)	−1685.900 (−0.952)	−50.962[a] (−1.963)	32.387 (0.341)	0.236	2.776
37	47	4.121 (0.353)		−9.126 (−0.236)	9.924[c] (3.642)	−3965.700 (−1.245)	18.193 (0.381)	213.800[c] (3.601)	0.326	3.231
39	21	53.146[b] (2.062)	−68.402 (−0.404)	−17.798 (−0.349)	3.452 (0.341)	−1487.100 (−0.720)	−36.132 (−0.395)	19.582 (0.087)	0.325	1.125
All manufacturing	1003	15.068[c] (6.955)	61.920[c] (3.240)	1.212 (0.162)	−0.119 (−0.477)	−1776.900[b] (−2.010)	−30.006[c] (−2.879)	71.307	0.068	12.154

[a] Coefficient statistically significantly different from zero at the 0.90 level of significance; two-tailed test.
[b] Coefficient statistically significantly different from zero at the 0.95 level of significance; two-tailed test.
[c] Coefficient statistically significantly different from zero at the 0.99 level of significance; two-tailed test.

industries. If those two-digit industries that have high mean values of *STD.HRS* also tend to have high levels of "disequilibrium" overtime then a spurious positive coefficient would result. On the other hand, Brechling [9] also found a positive relationship between hours of work and "normal hours" in his study, which used aggregate British time-series data.

To test for the identity of the structure (the equality of the set of co-efficients) across industries we can now perform a standard analysis of covariance, or Chow test.[5] Since this methodology will be employed extensively throughout the chapter it is probably relevant to summarize it here.

Let Q_1 be the residual sum of squares from the overall regression. Suppose we then break the sample of n observations into j groups, with the number of observations in each group n_j being greater than the number of coefficients K to be estimated. Let Q_2 be the sum (over the j groups) of the residual sum of squares from the within group regressions. Let $Q_3 = Q_1 - Q_2$, the reduction in the residual sum of squares from dissaggregation. Then, under the hypothesis that the structure is constant across groups (all the corresponding coefficients in the within-group regressions are equal), the following ratio will have an F distribution with $(nK - K, n - k)$ degrees of freedom

$$f = \frac{Q_3/(nK - K)}{Q_2/(n - K)}$$

If this ratio is greater than the critical value F_ε (if there is a significant reduction in the residual sum of squares by disaggregation) then the hypothesis that the set of coefficients is equal across groups is rejected. Note that this analysis crucially assumes, of course, that the true disturbance terms are normally distributed with mean zero and constant variance-covariance matrix $\sigma^2 I$ for each group.

Essentially, we are testing to see if the residual sum of squares is significantly reduced by disaggregating the data. If it is, then the hypothesis of identical structure of coefficients across industries is rejected. If the disturbances are not homoscedastic, the above test is not strictly appropriate. The appendix to this chapter discusses this problem in more detail. It is found in this case that the variance of the error term is *not* constant across industries, however, this fact does *not* alter our rejection of the null hypothesis.

Calculation of the required F ratio here indicates that $F = 44.557$ with (105, 891) degrees of freedom. This obviously exceeds the critical value of F at the 0.995 level of significance, which is 1.36; and consequently, we reject

---

[5] See J. Johnston [37], pp. 136–138, and G. Chow [17], pp. 591–605.

the hypothesis that the set of estimated coefficients is identical across all the manufacturing industries.

This approach gives us no information, however, as to which industries' coefficients are causing the hypothesis of equality to be rejected. Casual empirical inspection of the *RATIO* coefficients might indeed lead one to belief that it is the sets of coefficients of only a few industries that are leading to this conclusion. One possible way to test this assertion is to estimate regressions across establishments within every possible pair of manufacturing industry groupings (120 in all) and then perform Chow tests to see which *pairs* of two-digit industries may be considered as having identical sets of coefficients. It should be cautioned that these tests are not all independent, since data for establishments in any one industry are used in fifteen of the tests. This nonindependence has two important implications: First nonrejection of the hypothesis for any group of pairs does not imply nonrejection of the hypothesis when all industries in the group are considered together. Second, this procedure need not lead to a transitive relation; it may be legitimate to aggregate industries 1 and 2 together and industries 2 and 3 together, but not to aggregate industries 1 and 3.

Nevertheless, this procedure does yield some useful insights and it was therefore followed. Table 5–2 summarizes the results of the analysis. An asterisk indicates that the null hypothesis that the sets of estimated coefficients are identical for the pair of industries could be rejected at the 0.95 level of significance. Correspondingly, a blank implies the hypothesis could not be rejected; that there appeared to be no significant differences between the sets of coefficients for the two industries.

The implications to be drawn from this table are varied. For only 37 of the 120 pairwise comparisons can we reject the null hypothesis that the sets of coefficients are identical for both industries in the pair. As might be expected from Table 5–1, the set of coefficients for the Apparel industry (S.I.C. 23) differs significantly from those of all other industries, while the set for the Transportation Equipment industry (S.I.C. 37) differs from those of two-thirds of the other industries. The Paper (S.I.C. 26); Stone, Clay, and Glass (S.I.C. 32); and Electrical Equipment (S.I.C. 36) industries' coefficient sets all differ from over one-third of the other industries. On the other hand, the sets of coefficients for the Lumber (S.I.C. 24) and Furniture (S.I.C. 25) industries appear to differ significantly only from those of the Apparel and Transportation Equipment industries. This lends support to our belief that the insignificance of the *RATIO* coefficients for the Furniture and Lumber industries in Table 5–1, may indicate only that there were not sufficient observations to conduct a meaningful analysis in these industries.

The importance of the first five industries mentioned above, in causing

Table 5–2. Manufacturing Industries: Pairwise Chow Tests

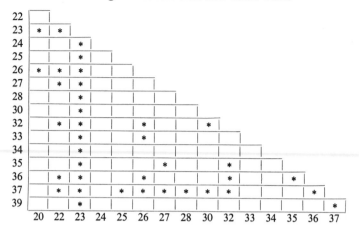

* Reject null hypothesis of equality of set of coefficients for the two industries at 0.95 level of significance.

S.I.C. Code—Industry Name

Group A	Group B
20—Food	23—Apparel
22—Textile	26—Paper
24—Lumber	32—Stone, clay, glass
25—Furniture	36—Electrical equipment
27—Printing	37—Transportation equipment
28—Chemical	
30　Rubber	
33—Primary metal	
34—Fabricated metal	
35—Machinery	
39—Misc. manufacturing	

the hypothesis of the quality of the set of coefficients across all manufacturing industries to be rejected, can be seen more clearly by dividing the sixteen manufacturing industries into a group containing only these five and a second group containing the other eleven. Table 5–3 repeats information found in Table 5–2, but considers only the within-group tests. The hypothesis of the equality of sets of coefficients can be rejected for *each* pairwise comparison among the five industries mentioned above (group B). The eleven industries contained in group A, however, with only two exceptions, appear to have homogeneous sets of coefficients on a pairwise basis.

Additionally, in 25 of the 55 pairwise comparisons between a group A and group B industry, the null hypothesis was rejected. The five industries

Table 5–3. Manufacturing Industries: Pairwise Chow Tests

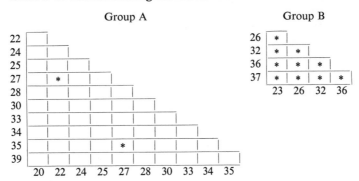

* Reject null hypothesis of equality of set of coefficients for the two industries at 0.95 level of significance.
Note: See note to Table 5–2 for S.I.C. industry code.

contained in group B do not appear to have any obvious technological characteristics that would lead one to expect (without looking at Table 5–1) that the results contained in Table 5–3 would occur.

Concepts of Equilibrium and the Problem of Omitted Variables

A distinction should be made between three different situations that a firm may find itself in: *long-run equilibrium*, which can be thought of as the stationary state of our dynamic model. *Short-run equilibrium* (but long-run disequilibrium), which is when the firm is optimally adjusting along the dynamic adjustment path of our model. *Short-run disequilibrium*, which is when the firm finds itself off of the optimal adjustment path due to such factors as mechanical breakdowns, rush orders, weather, emergencies, etc. Our empirical model is designed to handle only the first two situations, yet there is no doubt that a large, if not the major, component of overtime is due to short-run disequilibrium phenomenon. Thus the low R^2 values found in Table 5–1 are to be expected and are not discouraging.

A problem arises, however, in that we are omitting relevant unobservable explanatory variables from our regression equations. As indicated in Chapter 4, we have implicitly invoked the well-known result of Theil [68] that if the omitted variables are uncorrelated with the observed explanatory variables, then the estimated coefficients of the observed explanatory variables will remain unbiased. One may question whether this is a reasonable assumption.

In particular, we might argue that these disequilibrium components of over-time are related to establishment size. That is, we may tentatively hypothesize that large firms have greater flexibility than small firms. They may have stand-by equipment to which they can shift if one piece of equipment breaks down; they may be more easily able to absorb rush orders without recourse to overtime than small firms. What then disturbs the zero correlation assumption is that several of the observed explanatory variables are correlated with establishment size. In particular, large establishments are more likely to be unionized and tend to pay higher wages and fringe benefits. Consequently the coefficient estimates found in Table 5–1 may be biased.

Fortunately, the data permit us to classify establishments within industries into nine classes.[6] What we have essentially been arguing is that to account for the problem of omitted variables, we should allow the intercept term to vary with the establishment size. Consequently, the regression in Table 5–1 were rerun with (0, 1) dummy variables included for the nine size-code variables. These results are reported in Tables A5–1 (all variables but the size code) and 5–4 (the patterns of coefficients of the size code variables—henceforth denoted by ESC).[7]

Referring to Table A5–1 first, as expected, both the R^2 and F values increase substantially in most cases. The majority of the coefficients of the explanatory variables change only marginally from the coefficients in Table 5–1. Note however that the coefficient of *NEWSEN* is now negative and significant in an additional industry (Stone, Clay, and Glass—S.I.C. 32). Once again a Chow test indicates that the hypothesis of equality of the set of coefficients (including those of the ESC variables) across industries must be rejected.[8]

Consideration of the pattern of intercepts in Table 5–4 gives us some insight into the relationship of establishment size and "disequilibrium" overtime. Unfortunately, the relationship is obscured since many of the coefficients are not statistically significantly different from zero. What does emerge is that the pattern is *not* uniform across industries. Several industries (Food—20; Rubber—30; and Stone, Clay, and Glass—32) have the pattern we expected a priori: Large amounts of overtime for the smaller establishments and then fairly constant amounts for the other sizes. Others, such as Apparel—23, Furniture—25, and Electric Equipment—36 exhibit U-shaped

---

[6] These admittedly arbitrary classes are 0–25, 25–50, 50–100, 100–250, 250–500, 500–1000, 1000–2500, 2500–5000, and greater than 5000.

[7] All tables of regression results with an A preceding the identifying number are found in the appendix to this chapter.

[8] The F value is 29.351 with (225, 763) degrees of freedom compared with a critical value at the 0.995 level of 1.00.

Table 5–4. Intercept Varies with Establishment Size: Intercept Term

Industry

Size Class	20	22	23	24	25	26	27	28
ESC1	416.170[b]		118.850[c]	97.037	540.540[a]	−256.710	59.467	85.749
ESC2	196.380	−108.360	78.376[b]	24.906	458.120[a]	−248.390	24.516	8.466
ESC3	179.940	−27.956	84.648[c]	117.720	279.560	−135.350	98.615	30.401
ESC4	199.080	47.387	79.508[c]	232.450	314.320	−134.310	122.520	200.940[a]
ESC5	129.080	21.707	88.167[c]		330.720	−90.189	50.753	−6.112
ESC6	148.520	53.058	94.077[c]	−66.359	250.930	−100.860	−23.415	91.153
ESC7	220.370	67.883	95.283[b]	105.210	442.940	−28.045	122.480	18.670
ESC8	205.920	190.750	116.240[a]		490.230[a]	225.400	35.595	
ESC9		−148.290					44.650	
Constant				155.200				−89.075

Size Class	30	32	33	34	35	36	37	39
ESC1	72.137	571.670[c]		9.441	−46.569	−8.338	−1061.500[a]	224.330
ESC2	−9.880	444.580[b]	−86.056	131.290	116.870	−81.911	−129.600	263.370
ESC3	−1.012	255.380	172.750[a]	72.253	32.996	−111.230		161.560
ESC4	−95.245	320.130[a]	85.597	−25.444	168.580	−60.514		436.320
ESC5	−72.021	296.580	88.751	26.071	28.784	−52.404	−63.819	275.660
ESC6		281.640	74.181	74.836	−4.360	−36.732	−83.453	519.680
ESC7	−41.197	288.950	12.084		15.114	−2.810	8.240	225.280
ESC8		372.330	−6.120	81.387	−50.913	12.682	51.826	
ESC9					−53.034		−37.504	
Constant	−156.480[a]		248.190[a]	166.340				

[a] Coefficient statistically significantly different from zero at 0.90 level of significance; two-tailed test.
[b] Coefficient statistically significantly different from zero at 0.95 level of significance; two-tailed test.
[c] Coefficient statistically significantly different from zero at 0.99 level of significance; two-tailed test.
(For remaining coefficients see Table A5–1)

patterns, while in the Paper and Pulp—26 and Transportation Equipment—37 industries overtime appears to increase with establishment size. This latter result may be due to the large firms in the Transportation Equipment industry being concentrated in automobile manufacturing, with its previously noted seasonal pattern of excessive overtime. The remaining industries appear to have quite irregular patterns of behavior. While caution must be observed in interpreting these results due to the small sample sizes and consequently often insignificant coefficients, it is obvious that the relationship between overtime and establishment size is not as simple as one would expect a priori. This relationship will be investigated further in a later section.

The Simultaneity Problem

Our work in Chapter 3 advanced the argument that the ratio of "new" to "senior" workers is itself an endogenous variable and hence to avoid simultaneous equation bias in the estimates of the coefficients of equation (5.1a), the system of equations (2) should be estimated simultaneously.

$$OT = F(RATIO, STD.HRS, WAGE, ABSEN, NEWSEN, UNION)$$
$$(5.2a)$$

$$NEWSEN = G(RATIO, STD.HRS, WAGE, ABSEN, LABSEN, UNION)$$
$$(5.2b)$$

Here $LABSEN$ is a variable which represents the ratio of total labor services to the number of senior workers employed. The system of equations (5.2) is exactly identified and two-stage least squares may therefore be used to estimate it. There are two reasons, however, for questioning the usefulness of employing this methodology. First, the coefficient of $NEWSEN$ was not statistically significantly different from zero in the majority of the ordinary least square regressions. Second, since no theoretically appropriate measure of the metaphysical concept of total labor services was available, we were forced to use total man-hours paid for as a proxy. It is easy to see then, that implicitly $LABSEN$ can be written $(NEWSEN + 1)$ (observed annual hours per man). The correlation between $NEWSEN$ and $LABSEN$ is obviously extremely high; in effect we are *almost* regressing $NEWSEN$ on itself. That is, incorporating the notation of Chapter 3,

$$LABSEN = \frac{M_1 H_1 + M_2 H_2}{M_1 + M_2} = \left(\frac{M_1 + M_2}{M_2}\right) H_0 = (NEWSEN + 1)(H_0)$$

since $H_0 = (M_1 H_1 + M_2 H_2)/(M_1 + M_2)$. Here M_1 and M_2 represent the number of new and senior workers employed; H_1 and H_2 represent the *annual* hours per man worked for members of each class; and H_0 represents observed annual hours per man. The high correlation between *LABSEN* and *NEWSEN* occurs, because the bulk of annual hours per man are straight-time hours, which do not vary much across establishments.

Nevertheless to be consistent with our model, two-stage least square regressions were conducted and the equations discussed in the previous two sections reestimated. The results are found in Tables A5–2, A5–3, A5–4 and A5–5 in the appendix to this chapter.[9] Turning first to the *NEWSEN* equation, Table A5–2, as expected the R^2 are close to unity and *LABSEN* is by far the most important explanatory variable (the constancy of the coefficient across industries indicates that the regression is bordering on an identity). Somewhat surprising, given this fact, is that in 6 of the 16 industries the *RATIO* coefficient is negative and statistically significant. A negative coefficient for *RATIO* is predicted from the dynamic theory when $\gamma_2 K \leq 1$ and the coefficients of *NEWSEN* for these 6 industries in Table 5–1 indicate that this condition is met.[10]

Turning next to the overtime equations, in both the case when the intercept is constant (Table A5–3) and when it is allowed to shift with the ESC (Table A5–4 and A5–5), we find that the coefficients are virtually identical to the coefficients in the corresponding OLS equations. The primary difference in results is that the *RATIO* coefficient for Paper—26 and Printing—27 increases substantially, while that for Primary Metals—33 decreases slightly in both sets of regressions. The major conclusion that we draw from this analysis is therefore that the OLS results are probably adequate for policy purposes. Hence, in the remainder of both this chapter and the next we confine ourselves to using single equation methods.

Establishment Size and the Overtime Decision

We argued in a previous section that the intercept term should be allowed to vary with establishment size to capture the effects of the omitted variables. Several additional factors lead us now to argue that the coefficients of the other explanatory variables should also be allowed to vary across size classes of establishments within an industry.

---

[9] The *NEWSEN* equations when the intercept varies with ESC are not reported there since they add no additional insights.

[10] See footnote 17 in Chapter 3 for an explanation of why this is true.

First note that our underlying theory, in spite of its inclusion of several institutional features, is still based upon an idealized neoclassical world with substitutability of factors. There may be, however, indivisibilities inherent in small firms which prevent them from making some marginal decisions (i.e., what does a small firm do if its optimal employment level is 4.5 full-time employees?) In addition, there may be technical constraints in the production process, independent of absolute establishment size, which prevent the substitution of hours for men: Integrated assembly line operations often require a fixed number of men per shift, union rules may require a fixed number of men per crew, fixed men–machine ratios may exist. All these factors indicate that substitution may indeed be limited. We might initially expect that, in general, large firms have greater flexibility and are more able to make marginal decisions, and consequently that the significance and size of the *RATIO* coefficient would increase with ESC. Alternatively though, if it is the large firms that have production processes with the cited technical constraints, the reverse may be true.

To test whether the structure is constant across size classes, the eight manufacturing industries with the largest number of observations were each segmented by establishment size into three or more subgroups. Classifications were determined primarily by data considerations, although some attempt was made to make similar divisions across industries. The failure to accomplish this exactly is not disturbing since a firm, of say one hundred employees, may be considered "small" in one industry and "large" in a second depending upon the technical constraints discussed above.

For each industry, regressions were run within each subgroup and the results are reported in Table 5–5. Again, within each industry, a Chow test was conducted; and in five of the eight industries the null hypothesis that the whole set of coefficients was invariant across the different size groups was *rejected.* (These results are summarized in the table below.) Moreover in two of the three cases where the hypothesis was not rejected (Food—20 and Machinery—35), it appears at first glance that the *RATIO* coefficient varies

Industry	F Value	Degrees of Freedom	Action
20	1.619	(14,56)	Not reject at 90% level
22	2.341	(21,109)	Reject at 95% level
23	2.159	(21,98)	Reject at 95% level
32	2.189	(21,80)	Reject at 95% level
33	2.479	(12,59)	Reject at 95% level
34	2.231	(12,74)	Reject at 95% level
35	1.015	(14,58)	Not reject at 90% level
36	1.458	(14,40)	Not reject at 90% level

across the different size classes of establishments, although a formal statistical test of the difference between *RATIO* coefficients of the different size classes does not support this conjecture. Only in the case of the Electrical Equipment industry (36) does the structural relationship appear to be homogeneous for all size classes of establishments.

Consideration of the patterns of the size and significance of the *RATIO* coefficients across industries, indicates that only two industries (32 and 33) have the pattern we initially expected of the *RATIO* coefficient being largest and most significant for the largest class of establishments. In the Apparel industry (23) the *RATIO* coefficient is positive and significant only for establishments with *less* than one hundred employees, while in the Electric Equipment industry (36), the *RATIO* coefficient is almost identical across size classes. The remaining four industries exhibit varied patterns.

No simple explanation seems to exist that totally explains these results. Certainly the factors mentioned at the start of this section must play an important role. An alternative hypothesis that has been suggested to us, is that only firms with large amounts of overtime will be concerned with marginal decisions. For example, management may not consider the extra costs involved in scheduling overtime until perhaps over two hours a week per man must be paid for. However, a check of the mean value of overtime within each subclass indicates that this is probably not the case. In fact, in four of the eight industries (Food; Stone, Clay, and Glass; Primary Metals; and Fabricated Metals), it is the establishment size classes with the *smallest* amount of overtime that have the largest and most significant *RATIO* coefficient in the industry. It is actually conceivable that the direction of causation runs the opposite way: Establishments that are rational make the relevant marginal decisions and consequently have less overtime.

The groupings used in the above analysis are somewhat arbitrary and it would be desirable to further subdivide each industry into the original nine classes of establishments. The limited size of our samples prevents us from doing this since we would rapidly run out of degrees of freedom. Given, however, that we are primarily concerned with the coefficient of the *RATIO* variable and that the coefficients of the other explanatory variables are often insignificant, an alternative approach is to run a single regression within each industry allowing the intercept and *RATIO* coefficients to vary with establishment size, while constraining all other coefficients to be constant within the industry. That is, define dummy variables D_j such that

$$D_j = \begin{cases} 1 & \text{if the establishment is in } ESC_j \quad j = 1, \ldots, 9 \\ 0 & \text{otherwise} \end{cases}$$

Table 5-5. Basic Model: Data Disaggregated by Establishment Size Class (t ratios in parentheses)

$$OT = b_0 + b_1 RATIO + b_2 STD.HRS + b_3 WAGE + b_4 NEWSEN + b_5 ABSEN + b_6 UNION$$

Industry Number	Number of Observations	RATIO	STD.HRS	WAGE	NEWSEN	ABSEN	UNION	Constant	R^2	F
20 Total	77	26.398[b] (2.299)	16.241 (0.099)	−51.579[a] (−1.688)	0.079 (0.083)	−3127.400 (−1.041)	−32.564 (−0.754)	179.680 (1.096)	0.134	1.816
20 ESC(1-3)	29	22.719 (0.811)	101.300 (0.428)	−103.880 (−1.388)	0.162 (0.972)	−1074.800 (−0.731)	−78.220 (−0.835)	264.900 (1.080)	0.245	1.189
20 ESC(4-5)	24	48.616[c] (4.166)		−42.298 (−1.379)	0.034 (0.393)	−6906.800[c] (−2.916)	65.898 (1.502)	−2.388 (−0.036)	0.543	4.277
20 ESC(6-8)	24	16.574 (1.029)		−30.452 (−0.684)	−2.424 (−0.384)	−156.870 (−0.035)	−46.950 (−0.614)	200.420 (1.374)	0.111	0.448
22 Total	137	29.898[c] (3.317)	128.290 (1.512)	−57.444 (−1.013)	0.046 (0.528)	−6566.200[a] (−1.834)	−39.371[a] (−1.699)	69.336 (0.505)	0.112	2.727
22 ESC(1-4)	30	49.778[a] (1.713)		2.388 (0.018)	0.170 (0.861)	−892.46 (−0.016)	−13.049 (−0.505)	−47.821 (0.185)	0.128	0.706
22 ESC(5)	41	15.303 (1.191)	136.170 (1.214)	12.492 (0.192)	0.042 (0.374)	−2263.600 (−0.303)	−27.026 (−0.567)	−17.852 (−0.084)	0.079	0.438
22 ESC(6)	38	46.789[b] (2.612)	117.390 (1.315)	−26.626 (−0.214)	−1.738 (−0.587)	−9527.100[b] (−2.559)	−76.338[b] (−2.557)	−6.835 (−0.024)	0.398	3.413
22 ESC(7-8)	28	46.330[b] (2.083)		−316.220 (−1.349)	23.818 (0.120)	−9087.000 (−1.075)	−15.073 (−0.304)	636.280 (1.442)	0.387	2.771
23 Total	126	5.137[c] (3.737)	−28.108[b] (−2.109)	7.738 (0.795)	−0.041[b] (−2.340)	−2028.100 (−0.589)	−35.249[b] (−2.639)	80.023[c] (3.255)	0.204	5.090
23 ESC(1-3)	35	5.257[c] (3.501)	−34.112 (−1.107)	21.556 (1.307)	−0.031 (−1.052)	−1396.900 (−0.329)	−31.155 (−1.185)	46.288 (0.857)	0.471	4.159
23 ESC(4)	24	−9.910 (−1.012)	12.413 (0.360)	−67.927[b] (−2.013)	−0.056 (−1.113)	−2361.200 (−0.179)	50.702 (1.107)	191.620[b] (2.452)	0.244	0.914
23 ESC(5)	29	−0.113 (−0.022)	−4.713 (−0.176)	1.266 (0.038)	−0.058 (−1.397)	2257.400 (0.211)	−26.143 (−0.840)	94.084 (1.529)	0.140	0.594
23 ESC(6-9)	38	−0.208 (−0.018)	−30.881 (−0.810)	−16.329 (−0.699)	−0.048 (−0.766)	−1022.900 (−0.757)	−39.022 (−1.067)	170.380[b] (2.164)	0.185	1.170
32 Total	108	11.029 (1.091)	−39.457 (−0.271)	−80.680[b] (−2.264)	−0.080 (−0.823)	6937.400 (0.512)	19.542 (0.341)	378.190[b] (2.189)	0.053	0.947
32 ESC(1-3)	17	31.418 (0.632)		−88.640 (−0.549)	−0.056 (−0.293)	−2895.000 (−0.188)	33.551 (0.145)	275.900 (1.185)	0.105	0.258
32 ESC(4)	28	−6.982 (−0.257)	−50.554 (−0.303)	11.795 (0.163)	270.980[a] (1.734)		−134.760 (−1.040)	374.570 (1.358)	0.175	0.993
32 ESC(5)	26	−11.987		−113.180	49.292	1303.000	145.940	396.230	0.229	1.189

Category	No.	N	(1)	(2)	(2a)	(3)	(4)	(5)	(6)	R²	F
ESC(5)	32		(−0.438)	(−1.390)		(0.670)	(0.852)	(1.263)	(1.543)		
ESC(6–9)	33	37	26.812[a] (1.895)	14.822 (0.274)		351.590[b] (2.679)	9114.000[c] (2.805)		−15.789 (−1.082)	0.356	4.415
Total	33	77	19.727[b] (2.120)	−61.798 (−1.656)		0.226[a] (1.710)	1676.300 (0.370)	−34.134 (−0.786)	327.940[c] (3.461)	0.110	1.746
ESC(1–4)	33	20	11.555 (0.575)	64.893 (0.528)		0.021 (0.072)	1221.200 (0.168)	−28.877 (−0.313)	39.949 (0.137)	0.116	0.366
ESC(5–6)	33	26	−8.190 (−0.408)	−106.260 (−1.525)		279.440[a] (1.796)	7676.100[b] (2.101)	220.920[a] (1.766)	356.800 (1.662)	0.358	2.232
ESC(7–8)	34	31	55.802 (5.247)	−79.695[a] (−1.901)		468.888[b] (2.268)	−2693.400[a] (−1.928)	32.513 (0.571)	65.376 (0.409)	0.594	7.323
Total	34	92	26.392[b] (2.489)	−53.310 (−1.635)		0.065 (0.581)	−3139.300 (−1.218)	−8.440 (−0.217)	212.920[b] (2.385)	0.101	1.936
ESC(1–3)	34	31	35.182 (1.262)	−45.266 (−0.606)		0.063 (0.394)	−6373.800 (−1.373)	32.657 (0.400)	174.480 (0.876)	0.141	0.821
ESC(4–5)	34	37	33.579[b] (2.254)	−28.893 (−0.680)		−0.476 (−0.091)	−562.670 (−0.160)	−7.852 (−1.478)	68.629 (0.509)	0.169	1.263
ESC(6–8)	35	24	16.353 (0.967)	−108.040[a] (−1.741)		25.987 (1.324)	4665.100[b] (2.075)	−238.800[b] (−2.008)	646.850[c] (3.623)	0.398	2.383
Total	35	79	33.695[c] (3.784)	−40.338 (−1.262)	127.190 (1.099)	−2.563 (−0.820)	2882.50 (−0.843)	−15.809 (−0.843)	83.480 (0.538)	0.222	3.428
ESC(1–3)	35	26	20.535 (0.852)	−61.204 (0.656)		−4.103 (−0.866)	−1852.30 (−0.291)	−6.910 (0.057)	332.880 (1.505)	0.099	0.437
ESC(4–6)	35	27	51.839[c] (3.300)	−15.970 (−0.332)	168.850 (1.190)	4.377 (0.446)	−223.210 (−0.028)	34.347 (0.433)	−145.830 (−0.580)	0.425	2.459
ESC(7–9)	36	26	23.868[a] (1.943)	−65.679 (−1.237)		−120.890 (−0.945)	−3278.00 (−0.632)	7.361 (0.132)	306.150[a] (2.073)	0.269	1.469
Total	36	61	32.481[c] (3.635)	4.573 (0.225)	−36.595 (0.58)	4.302 (0.521)	−1685.900 (−0.952)	−50.672[a] (−1.963)	32.387 (0.341)	0.236	2.776
ESC(1–4)	36	19	35.898[a] (1.770)	53.025 (1.009)		7.476 (0.597)	1527.300 (0.209)	−73.190 (−1.154)	−150.610 (−0.871)	0.325	1.253
ESC(5–6)	36	19	33.866[a] (1.949)	−20.515 (0.665)		66.273 (1.072)	−898.250 (−0.332)	−52.070 (−1.029)	17.857 (0.158)	0.254	0.883
ESC(7–9)		23	31.251[b] (2.237)	−34.711 (−0.979)	−26.411 (−0.452)	58.748 (0.842)	−1187.400 (−0.463)	−46.449 (−1.018)	150.040 (1.259)	0.380	1.632

[a] Coefficient statistically significantly different from zero at 0.90 level of significance; two-tailed test.
[b] Coefficient statistically significantly different from zero at 0.95 level of significance; two-tailed test.
[c] Coefficient statistically significantly different from zero at 0.99 level of significance; two-tailed test.
Establishment Size Codes (ESC): (1) 1–25, (2) 25–50, (3) 50–100, (4) 100–24, (5) 250–500, (6) 500–1000, (7) 1000–2500, (8) and (9) greater than 2500.

Then the regression run is

$$OT = \sum_{j=1}^{9} \gamma_j D_j + \sum_{j=1}^{9} \alpha_j D_j RATIO + \sum_{j=1}^{5} \beta_j X_j \qquad (5.3)$$

where the X_j are the other explanatory variables. The intercept is allowed to vary in order to capture the effect of the omitted variables, as discussed earlier.

Equation (5.3) was estimated for all sixteen industries; the estimated intercepts and coefficients of the $RATIO$ variables are presented in Table 5–6, the remaining coefficients are relegated to Table A5–6 in the appendix. It should be pointed out that, especially for the eight industries with the fewest observations, collinearity problems exist. In particular, the correlation between D_j and $D_j RATIO$ is extremely high in those cases where there are only a few observations in size-class j. While multicollinearity does not bias the coefficients, it does drastically increase their standard errors and this should be kept in mind when interpreting the results.[11]

Considering the results in Table 5–6, it is immediately obvious that the coefficient of the $RATIO$ variable varies across size classes. A formal statistical test of the equality of these coefficients across size classes within an industry could be devised but is computationally difficult. More interesting from a policy point of view, is simply to ask for what size firms is the $RATIO$ coefficient positive and significant? It unfortunately appears that there is no consistent pattern either within or across industries. Moreover, observing the results for the eight industries with the largest number of observations, it appears also that the groupings used in Table 5–5 were not all appropriate. Again, we also find that the sets of intercepts yield no consistent patterns across industries.

The Effect of Unions

Previously we attempted to capture the affects of union rules calling for overtime pay for weekend and holiday work by including a collective bargaining dummy variable in the regressions. This method is inadequate, however, to

---

[11] One possible way to avoid this problem is to constrain the intercept term to be equal across size classes. But then in cases where there are only a few observations in a given size class, a large (or small) $RATIO$ coefficient may indicate only that size class has a large (or small) disequilibrium component of overtime. Empirically this is what resulted when this methodology was employed and hence the results of this analysis are not presented here.

capture the total affect of unions on overtime. Whether or not a firm is unionized affects the other explanatory variables: Unionized firms tend to pay higher wages, have higher fringe benefits, allow more paid sick leave, etc. These factors will be captured in the regressions although not directly attributed to the unions. Unions may, in addition, crucially alter the structure of the underlying relationship. For example union rules concerning layoffs, the existence of stand-by crews, or the number of men in a crew, may alter the optimal employment–hours combination, as well as the marginal affects of the other explanatory variables. Hence, it is appropriate to test if the structural relation is different between unionized and nonunionized firms.

The eight industries with the largest numbers of observations were again each divided into two subgroups, depending upon whether the majority of the establishments' production workers were covered by collective bargaining. Within each industry, regressions were estimated for both the unionized and nonunionized subgroups, as well as the total sample, and the results are tabulated in Table A5–7.[12] Again Chow tests were conducted and the results are uniform across industries: The null hypothesis that the set of coefficients was the same for both unionized and nonunionized establishments in the same industry could *not* be rejected.[13] The general conclusion to be drawn from this section then, is that while unions may influence the level of overtime, they do not appear to affect the underlying structural relationship.

Also, it is interesting to note that in Table A5–7, the *RATIO* coefficient for the regression run over unionized firms in the Stone, Clay, and Glass industry (32) is positive and *significant*. This was one of the four industries for which this coefficient was not significant in the overall regressions (see Table 5–1).

Component Industries and Overtime Behavior

The final question to be considered in this chapter is whether for the purposes of studying the overtime decision it is "correct" to aggregate component three-digit industries into two-digit industries. The two-digit industry classification is constructed broadly along *product* lines. The underlying problem

---

[12] Regressions were also estimated allowing the intercept to vary with ESC and the results were similar and hence not reported here.

[13] The following values of the F ratio (with corresponding degrees of freedom) were all too low to reject the null hypothesis at the 90 percent level:

S.I.C. 20 $F = 1.564$ (6, 65)   S.I.C. 22 $F = 1.675$ (6, 125)
S.I.C. 23 $F = 1.505$ (6, 114)   S.I.C. 32 $F = 1.186$ (6, 96)
S.I.C. 33 $F = 1.023$ (5, 67)   S.I.C. 34 $F = 0.261$ (5.82)
S.I.C. 35 $F = 0.975$ (6, 67)   S.I.C. 36 $F = 1.437$ (6, 49)

Table 5–6. Intercept and Ratio Coefficients Vary With ESC

Ratio

Size Class	20	22	23	Industry 24	25	26	27	28
ESC1	280.15[c]		37.09[c]	−19.42	53.94	47.74	12.29	
ESC2	−38.73	−20.21	0.27	60.01	31.28	−191.58	11.12	13.98
ESC3	18.70	−5.33	5.18[c]	−554.63[a]		140.67	−157.54[b]	24.15
ESC4	45.24[a]	106.77[c]	3.31	−27.47	−81.99	67.25	−216.11[b]	−11.55
ESC5	46.08[a]	20.55[a]	0.38	13.91	72.78	97.75	106.09[c]	−40.99
ESC6	30.81	47.15[b]	−3.08	45.57	−5.68	53.87	−325.15[a]	43.21
ESC7	18.79	49.34[b]	16.11	−68.82	143.11[a]	204.16	29.84	−23.27
ESC8	−61.99	117.32[a]	24.89[c]		218.30	131.96	811.85[b]	109.98[c]
ESC9		4.99					−403.59	

Intercept

Size Class	20	22	23	Industry 24	25	26	27	28
ESC1	−666.48[a]		−48.71		444.05		369.07[b]	−132.45
ESC2	461.77[b]	143.84	93.48	−356.60	487.67	971.46	428.64[b]	
ESC3	182.73	189.22	79.03[c]	1731.00[a]	390.54	−354.70	1346.20[b]	−153.04
ESC4	57.24	−225.25	80.26[a]	230.98	859.00	1.05	1510.30[b]	215.08
ESC5	11.48	102.03	103.97[c]	−170.37	161.42	−119.60	−78.21	182.60
ESC6	70.42	28.88	128.11[c]	−485.48	451.39	150.89	1861.80[b]	−256.73
ESC7	219.41	35.81	27.16[b]	163.20		−643.66	365.38[a]	148.22
ESC8	759.62					−11.16	−2864.70[b]	−997.66[b]
ESC9							3010.90	
Constant			407.40					−24.336

[a] Coefficient statistically significantly different from zero at 0.90 level of significance; two-tailed test.
[b] Coefficient statistically significantly different from zero at 0.95 level of significance; two-tailed test.
[c] Coefficient statistically significantly different from zero at 0.99 level of significance; two-tailed test.

Coefficients

30	32	33	34	35	36	37	39
	344.82[a]		50.775	−114.24	7.62[a]	−7196.60[b]	−596.03[b]
92.22	42.01	90.17	77.332	9.73	17.72	37.25	4.37
89.17[a]	29.93	−30.34	24.175	70.19	0.36		39.26
−59.41	−9.81	191.54[c]	39.65[a]	70.21[c]	36.87[b]	83.47[b]	36.35
26.84	−27.03	30.69[b]	11.160	13.49	11.57	−4.46	1.81
318.54	11.88	−17.04	7.550	42.39[a]	31.31[a]	−26.82	912.72
90.33	70.31[a]	19.06	1.100	17.95	26.49	−22.91	−368.48
104.80[a]		45.25	6.000	25.16	39.34	−32.22	
		60.07[c]		55.36	−183.63	2.07	

Coefficients

30	32	33	34	35	36	37	39
	−411.36		−319.75	628.99			3198.90[c]
240.01	365.14	−141.94	−291.88	222.85	164.23	−195.26	130.80
−305.51	171.87	622.35[b]	−98.94	−158.51	221.94		−254.71
462.10	443.43	−313.72	−273.91	−83.36	93.31	−277.39	
−42.22	489.82	203.89	−68.85	119.50	238.38	2.20	5.38
1370.30	301.89	516.79[c]	6.85	−82.10	150.43	60.80	−4138.70
−371.50	110.14	253.81		90.35	204.72	149.97	2765.10
−483.06	432.78	111.61		−11.21	151.82	275.68	
				−175.41	1138.00		
		42.98	340.96				

Table 5–7. Intercept and Ratio Coefficients Varying Across Three-Digit Industries

Industry Number	Intercept	RATIO	Industry Number	Intercept	RATIO
201	120.3	48.16^a	331	373.9^b	11.46
202	+412.8^a	−83.68^b	332	−201.6	+41.10
203	+141.3	−45.64	333	+176.1	
204	−619.2^a	+130.51^b	335	−90.8	+8.53
205	+143.6	−41.45	336	+437.4	−115.19
206	+57.9	−33.18	339	+184.5	−20.52
207	+175.8	−46.89			
208	+22.7	−20.72			
209	−306.5^b	+48.03^b			
221	382.8^b	16.58	341	257.4	26.50
222	−12.5	+9.81	342	−56.4	+2.95
223	−779.7^b	+201.70^b	343	+14.4	−26.53
225	−233.2^a	+39.40	344	+25.2	+0.50
226	−553.6^a	+182.10^c	345	+774.5^a	−98.63^a
227	+518.1	−104.60	346	+14.0	−15.81
228	+116.5	−24.60	347	−209.8	+0.38
229	−4.4	−0.50	348	+190.9	−14.19
			349	−23.7	−1.12
231	56.0	0.53	351	1.19	32.14
232	+95.5^b	−19.30^a	352	+209.7	−37.98
233	+5.3	+5.33	353	+75.7	+10.95
234	+10.2	+1.14	354	+169.3	−14.00
235	−155.0	+73.16^a	355	−141.4	+25.91
236	−88.3	+27.85^a	356	+131.3	−13.16
237		+10.72	357	−198.4	+39.73
238	+0.6	+6.99	358	+81.3	−5.46
239	−25.2	+5.40	359	+73.8	−12.23
321	493.2^a	−19.59	361	−300.3^a	95.83^c
322	+126.4	−5.25	362	+199.6	−49.03
323		−7.20	363	+512.8^c	−108.97^c
324	−143.8	−6.44	364	+463.5^c	−102.04^c
325	−687.4	+114.58^a	365	+373.3^a	−8236^b
326		+3.65	366	+325.4^b	−64.34^b
327	−521.4^a	+139.53^c	367	+257.4^a	−52.45^b
328	−300.9	+98.12	369	+30.7	−6.75

^{a} Coefficient statistically significant from zero at 0.90 level of significance.
^{b} Coefficient statistically significant from zero at 0.95 level of significance.
^{c} Coefficient statistically significant from zero at 0.99 level of significance.
Coefficients other than those of the three-digit industry ending in 1 are deviations from the corresponding coefficient for industry 1.

is that the structural relationship is expected to be invariant across firms using the same *productive process*—not firms that fall under the same *product classification*. Technical processes are far more homogeneous among firms within a three-digit industry than they are across three-digit industries within a given two-digit industry.[14] Consequently, we might expect that disaggregation is necessary.

With a larger sample, we would ideally like to estimate regressions over establishments within individual three- or four-digit industries and then test for structural differences (within a two-digit industry). The variance of the published mean values of overtime in component three-digit industries is large enough to suggest that either: (1) these differences exist, (2) the values of the explanatory variables varies across industries, or (3) the causes and consequently the level of "disequilibrium" overtime varies across these industries. Given our sample size, we are constrained, however, to a procedure similar to that used in a previous section. Define dummy variables d_i such that,

$$d_i \quad \begin{cases} 1 & \text{if the establishment is in a three-digit industry that ends in } i \\ & \hspace{4cm} (i = 2, \ldots, 9) \\ 0 & \text{otherwise} \end{cases}$$

Then the regression equation estimated is

$$OT = \alpha_1 + \sum_{i=2}^{9} \alpha_i d_i + b_1 \, RATIO + \sum_{i=2}^{9} b_i \, D_i \, RATIO + \sum_{i=1}^{5} \gamma_i X_i \quad (5.4)$$

where the X_i are again the other explanatory variables. In this formulation, α_1 and b_1 are the intercept and coefficient of the *RATIO* variable for the component three-digit industry that ends in 1. However α_i and b_i $(i = 2, \ldots, 9)$ now represent the *deviations* of the corresponding coefficients for the *i*th component industry from the values of α_1 and b_1.

Again noting that care must be exercised in analyzing the results due to the small samples and collinearity problem, equation (5.4) was estimated for each of the eight industries with the largest number of observations. The estimated intercept and *RATIO* coefficients are presented in Table 5–7. It should be obvious that component industries do *not* always exhibit identical behavior. Both the intercept and coefficient of the *RATIO* variable for the various component industries often differ significantly from the corresponding coefficients of "industry one." More important, the difference is not always only one of magnitude. For example, the coefficient of the *RATIO* variable

---

[14] The Stone, Clay, and Glass industry (32) is a prime example of this fact.

can be shown to be significantly negative for the dairy products industry (S.I.C. 202). It is also interesting to note that in the Stone, Clay, and Glass industry (S.I.C. 32), at least one component industry, the Concrete, Gypsum and Plaster industry, displays a large and statistically significantly positive *RATIO* coefficient. The aggregation of the continuous-process glass industries with this industry when studying overtime behavior, is obviously a mistake.

Summary

The principal finding of this chapter has been a confirmation of the role of the quasi-fixed labor costs in influencing the overtime–employment trade-off. In the majority of the two-digit manufacturing industries for which sufficient data are available to conduct the analysis (12 of 16), observed overtime hours per man have been shown to be significantly positively related to the ratio of weekly fixed employment costs per man to the overtime wage rate. This relationship is not invariant across the two-digit industries, however.

While caution must be observed in disaggregating the data further due to small sample sizes, several subsidiary findings are of interest: It appears that this relationship is not invariant across establishments of different size classes within a two-digit industry. Moreover, the relationship does not vary systematically with establishment size in any uniform way across industries. Different component three-digit industries within a given two-digit industry also often exhibit significantly different relationships between overtime per man and the ratio of weekly fixed labor costs per man to the overtime wage rate. These findings will obviously influence the implications for policy that will be drawn in Chapter 7. On the other hand, while unions may alter the amount of overtime per man worked, they do not appear to affect the underlying structural relationship between overtime and the explanatory variables.

Two other results should also be briefly mentioned. Contrary to our initial expectations, there appears to be no consistent relationship within industries, between establishment size and the disequilibrium component of overtime. It also appears that in the majority of the manufacturing industries, the relative wage rate of new workers is approximately equal to their relative productivity.

The existence of a qualitative relationship between annual overtime per man and the *RATIO* variable in itself does not lead to any policy recommendations. What is important to have are quantitative estimates of the impact of a change in the overtime premium on overtime and employment. Such estimates can be derived directly from our estimated regression coefficients and will be presented after we analyze the nonmanufacturing industries' data in the next chapter.

6 Overtime Behavior in U.S. Nonmanufacturing Industries, 1966

This chapter presents the results of our empirical investigation of intra-industry variations in observed annual overtime hours per man for the U.S. nonmanufacturing industries in 1966. It should be indicated that there are difficulties involved in using the B.L.S. survey data for establishments in these industries. First, in several of the nonmanufacturing industries, the concept of overtime pay does not conform closely to that of our theoretical models. For example, in portions of the transportation industry, drivers receive overtime pay if they exceed a certain mileage per day, independent of the number of hours they work. Secondly, the nonmanufacturing industries are not at all covered uniformly by the Fair Labor Standards Act [87], as the manufacturing industries are. Because of this, in our sample, three different classes of establishments will be listed as having zero overtime hours at premium pay: noncovered establishments that may work their employees overtime but do not pay them premium wages; noncovered establishments that choose to work their employees zero overtime but that would pay a premium rate, not necessarily equal to time-and-a-half, for any overtime hours; covered establishments that choose to schedule zero overtime for their employees but are required by law to pay an overtime premium of at least time-and-a-half for any overtime worked. It is impossible, given our data, to separate the establishments belonging to each of these classes and correspondingly to determine what is the relevant overtime premium facing any of these establishments. Consequently, it is necessary to eliminate all three classes of establishments from our sample and, as seen below in detail, this involves a reduction in our total sample size from about 2,529 to 1,275 nonmanufacturing establishments. As a result, the empirical results which follow *cannot* be generalized to the whole population of nonmanufacturing establishments.[1]

In contrast to these difficulties, there are several important reasons for undertaking the analysis of this data. First, there exists *no* published data on overtime for the nonmanufacturing industries comparable to that found in *Employment and Earning Statistics* [77] for the manufacturing industries.

---

[1] Since an increase in the overtime premium could not possibly decrease overtime in those establishments that have zero overtime, it may actually be desirable to eliminate them from the sample. That is, if there is a discontinuity in the relationship between overtime per man and the *RATIO* variable when overtime equals zero, inclusion of the zero overtime establishments may bias the estimated regression coefficient.

Hence no study, even at the aggregate level, has ever been undertaken of overtime behavior in the nonmanufacturing industries. Secondly, as observed by Fuchs [28], employment in the manufacturing industries is declining trend-wise relative to that of the nonmanufacturing industries, with the primary growth of employment occurring in the service industries (wholesale and retail trade; services; and finance, insurance, and real estate). Given the growing importance of this sector, behavior in it and the determinants of the behavior become increasingly important from a policy point of view. Finally, the 1962 and 1966 amendments to the Fair Labor Standards Act [87] extended the premium pay for overtime provisions of the act to cover a substantial number of previously uncovered nonmanufacturing workers.[2] Consequently, it becomes more meaningful to speak about the wisdom of increasing "the overtime premium" in these industries. These factors all suggest that a study using the nonmanufacturing data will be useful.

Since no published data on the mean levels or distribution of overtime are available for the nonmanufacturing industries, the distributions of overtime within an industry from our sample warrant presentation here.[3] Table 6–1 presents a breakdown of the data at approximately the two-digit level. For each industry, the total number of establishments and the number with positive amounts of overtime are presented. While the ratio of these two numbers varies across industries, as indicated above for the sample as a whole, only slightly more than 50 percent have positive amounts of overtime. This should be contrasted with the data for the manufacturing industries in which the comparable figure was over 95 percent.

Confining ourselves to those establishments with positive overtime, Table 6–2 presents the sample means and standard deviations of annual overtime per employee within an industry, for eight broader industry groups. These are the groupings used throughout most of the chapter, although it will be shown later that the estimated set of coefficients is not always identical across two-digit industries within such a group.

The Figures shown in Table 6–2 should *not* be taken as representative of the entire industry groups since they exclude the zero overtime establishments. Nevertheless they indicate that substantial amounts of overtime are being worked and that within-industry variance in overtime among these establishments is large. To show that this variance is at least partially due to the factors discussed in the preceding chapters is the task of this chapter. The remainder of this chapter therefore presents a statistical analysis of the data similar to that conducted with the manufacturing data.

---

[2] The 1966 amendments did not go fully into effect until 1968 and consequently would not have substantially affected the observation for 1966 that we are using.

[3] The sampling techniques used should be kept in mind, however.

Table 6–1. Distribution of Nonmanufacturing Data

Industry Name	S.I.C. Code	Number of Establishments	Establishments with Nonzero Overtime
Mining	10–14	38	37
General contractors	15	402	210
Heavy construction	16	28	26
Special trade contractors	17	78	49
Railroad transportation	40	45	43
Local transit	41	202	0
Motor freight	42	269	196
Water transportation	44	186	0
Air transportation	45	35	0
Pipelines and services	46, 47	23	0
Communications	48	21	19
Electric, gas, sanitary systems	49	167	165
Wholesale trade	50	340	244
Hardware stores	52	33	20
General stores	53	46	35
Food stores	54	65	41
Auto service	55	72	26
Apparel stores	56	24	10
Furniture stores	57	17	5
Restaurants	58	23	21
Misc. retail trade	59	50	14
Financial institutions, etc.	60–66	49	25
Hotels	70	30	13
Personal services	72	48	18
Misc. business services	73	36	27
Auto and misc. repair	75, 76	19	6
Amusements	78, 79	29	7
Medical services	80	71	16
Other services	81–89	13	5
Total nonmanufacturing data		2,529	1,275

Table 6–2. Distribution of Nonmanufacturing Data: Nonzero Overtime Establishments

Industry Name	S.I.C. Code	Number of Observations	Annual Mean Overtime Hours Per Man	Standard Deviation Overtime Hours Per Man
Mining	10–14	37	152.287	132.765
Construction	15–17	285	125.217	171.449
Transportation	40, 42	239	186.645	171.272
Utilities	48, 49	184	121.731	73.306
Wholesale trade	50	244	188.992	211.959
Retail trade	52–59	172	110.051	146.416
Financial	60–66	25	122.222	108.292
Services	70–89	89	89.819	115.160

The Basic Model

Essentially the same theoretical model as that developed for the manufacturing industries in Chapter 2 may be used as the basis for the empirical work conducted here. Indeed it is probably more relevant in the low-wage service and trade sectors to assume that the firm faces an infinitely elastic supply of labor at a given wage, than it is in the manufacturing industries.[4] The notion of the internal labor market is probably less relevant for the nonmanufacturing industries though. However, ignoring the dynamics of the adjustment process if a firm employs labor of different qualities at varying wage rates, an aggregation problem similar to that discussed in Chapter 3 will still exist since all we can observe is a weighted average of the hours of each class of workers. To account for this phenomenon we again include *NEWSEN*, the ratio of those employees who receive less than one week paid vacation a year to all other employees. Again the sign of this variable will indicate whether senior employees (as measured here) work longer hours than new employees.

There is an additional influence, however, that tends to build in a negative relationship between *NEWSEN* and overtime. Part-time workers make up a substantial part of the labor force (over 20 percent) in wholesale and retail trade and the service industries.[5] Most part-time workers receive short, if any, vacations. Hence we would expect that part-time workers would be classified in the class of "new" workers. Observed overtime per *man* would therefore tend to decrease as the number of new workers increased, if this increase was an increase in part-time employees. On the other hand, if full-time new workers tend to work longer hours than full-time senior workers, an increase in this component of new workers would increase observed overtime. Consequently, the relationship between observed overtime and *NEWSEN* may be obscured because we cannot distinguish between the two classes of new workers in the data.

Given this qualification, the basic model estimated is identical to that of the previous chapter.

$$OT = a_0 + a_1\,RATIO + a_2\,STD.HRS + a_3\,WAGE + a_4\,ABSEN \\ + a_5\,NEWSEN + a_6\,UNION \quad (6.1)$$

The results of estimating equation (6.1) for each of the eight major industry groups are found in Table 6–3. Again, the most striking conclusion

---

[4] See Cotterill [19] for a study using cross-section census SMSA data that indicates that the supply of labor in the retail trade industries is highly elastic.

[5] See Fuchs [28], Table 186, p. 68.

is that in six of the eight nonmanufacturing industry groups the coefficient of the *RATIO* variable is positive and statistically significantly different from zero at at least the 95 percent level of significance. The two industries in which it is not significant are the ones with the fewest observations, Financial Institutions and Mining. Moreover, payments into union welfare funds in a segment of the Mining industry are also a function of the number of tons of coal produced rather than the number of men employed. Given this particular method of financing fringe benefits, we would not expect our calculated *RATIO* variable to have a significant impact on overtime in this industry.

The coefficient of wage is negative in six of eight industries and significant in three. These negative coefficients may be capturing more than the demand side effect of the quit rate. In particular low wage firms in an industry may attract the lowest quality workers. Hence, to achieve a given level of labor services these workers must work longer hours and more overtime. As long as the total labor bill is not increased above the level that the firm would incur if it employed more productive labor at higher wages and fewer hours per man, the firm will not object to increased overtime.

NEWSEN is significant in only two of eight cases and positive in both of these cases. The positive coefficient, especially in low-wage retail trade may reflect a supply response on the part of new workers, that are more willing to accept overtime than are senior workers who earn higher wages. *ABSEN* is negative in six of eight industries and significant in two, a result again similar to the manufacturing industry results. This may once again indicate that the "variability of the absentee rate is positively related to its mean value for each establishment." Finally *STD.HRS* is mixed in sign, and primarily insignificant as is *UNION*, which is negative in six of eight industries.

It should be remarked that the results presented in Table 6–3 appear to be for the most part "better" than the comparable results for the manufacturing industries, in terms of the overall *F* statistics and the *t* statistics for the *RATIO* coefficients. This is not surprising when we consider that in addition to the larger sample sizes, there are likely to be fewer problems with fixed men–machine ratios, assembly line processes, etc. in the nonmanufacturing industries than in the manufacturing industries, which can prevent the postulated employment–hours trade-off from occurring. Moreover, as we shall indicate later, in most cases the production processes in the nonmanufacturing industries appear to be fairly homogeneous within industries, across establishments of different size classes. This would also tend to add to the significance of the coefficients of a regression estimated across all size classes of firms within a given industry.

The question again arises as to whether it is necessary to disaggregate the nonmanufacturing data into industry groupings. Once again an overall

Table 6–3. Basic Model: Ordinary Least Square Estimates (*t* ratios in parenthesis)

$$OT = a_0 + a_1 RATIO + a_2 STD.HRS + a_3 WAGE + a_4 NEWSEN + a_5 ABSEN + a_6 UNION$$

Industry	Number of Obstructions	RATIO	STD.HRS	WAGE	NEWSEN	ABSEN	UNION	Constant	R^2	F
Mining	37	0.343 (0.043)	-13.006 (-0.115)	-36.543 (-1.452)	0.091 (1.647)	-4183.400[a] (-1.919)	-53.270 (-1.213)	293.450[c] (2.357)	0.478	4.575
Construction	285	30.929[c] (5.933)	8.228 (0.226)	-26.134[b] (-2.300)	0.003 (0.253)	-3250.400 (-0.568)	-12.672 (-0.511)	113.150[b] (2.049)	0.128	6.813
Transportation	239	42.888[c] (5.325)	127.880 (0.791)	-36.951[a] (-1.797)	0.099[a] (1.880)	-1246.600 (-0.410)	-21.340 (-0.582)	-63.550 (-0.361)	0.139	6.239
Utilities	184	7.899[b] (2.048)	-65.203[b] (-1.971)	-9.957 (-0.791)	3.385 (0.121)	335.400 (0.425)	9.774 (0.795)	145.460[b] (2.268)	0.080	2.573
Wholesale trade	244	39.093[c] (6.436)	49.771 (0.836)	-102.440[c] (-5.679)	-0.030 (-0.424)	-3124.100[b] (-2.177)	-2.807 (-0.100)	205.710[c] (2.893)	0.240	12.491
Retail trade	172	35.101[c] (4.698)	53.081[a] (1.766)	-9.852 (-0.572)	0.168[c] (2.863)	703.200 (0.429)	-39.863[a] (-1.662)	-48.844 (-1.011)	0.177	5.927
Services	89	40.370[c] (4.438)	-34.343 (-0.955)	12.580 (0.849)	-0.014 (-0.303)	-2121.900 (-1.392)	-35.209 (1.367)	-39.875 (-0.885)	0.240	4.324
Financial institutions	25	14.673 (1.142)	-56.608 (-1.079)	22.091 (0.379)	-7.180 (-0.559)	-717.530 (-0.297)	108.000 (1.617)	30.064 (0.240)	0.327	1.461
All nonman- ufacturing	1275	29.814[c] (12.594)	33.007[a] (1.880)	-26.887[c] (-4.857)	0.046[c] (3.436)	-3685.800[c] (-6.521)	-15.893 (-1.518)	62.982[c] (2.806)	0.130	31.696

[a] Coefficient statistically significantly different from zero at the 0.90 level of significance; two-tailed test.
[b] Coefficient statistically significantly different from zero at the 0.95 level of significance; two-tailed test.
[c] Coefficient statistically significantly different from zero at the 0.99 level of significance; two-tailed test.

regression using all 1,275 nonmanufacturing observations was estimated and the results listed at the bottom of Table 6–3. Aggregation drastically increased the significance of most of the coefficients as well as the overall F statistic. To test for the identity of the set of coefficients across industries we then performed a standard Chow test. Calculation of the required F ratio indicates that $F = 20.59$ with (49,1219) degrees of freedom. This is obviously larger than the critical value of F at the 0.995 level of significance which is 1.53 and hence we reject the null hypothesis that the set of estimated coefficients is identical across industry groups.

The test does not tell us which industries' sets of coefficients are causing the hypothesis of equality to be rejected. Casual empirical inspection of the *RATIO* coefficients indeed leads one to believe that at least several of the industries might have quite similar structures and could consequently be aggregated together. As noted in the previous chapter, a possible way to test this assertion is to estimate regressions across establishments within every possible pair of nonmanufacturing industry groups (28 in all) and then perform Chow tests to see which *pairs* of industry groups may be considered as having identical sets of coefficients.

When utilized with the manufacturing industry data, this procedure yielded several useful insights and consequently it was followed again. Table 6–4 reports the results of the analysis; an asterisk indicates that the

Table 6–4. Nonmanufacturing Industries:
Pairwise Chow Test

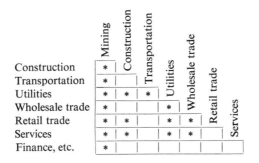

null hypothesis that the sets of estimated coefficients are identical for both industries could be rejected at the 0.95 level of significance. Correspondingly, a blank implies that the hypothesis could not be rejected; that there appeared to be no significant difference between the sets of coefficients of the two industries.

The implications to be drawn from this table are varied. As might be expected from Table 6–3, the Mining industry's relationship differs significantly from those of all the other industries. On the other hand, the set of coefficients for the Finance industry does *not* appear to be significantly different from the set of any other industry, except Mining. The insignificance of the *RATIO* coefficient for this industry may indicate, therefore, only that there were not sufficient observations to conduct a meaningful analysis. The set of coefficients for the Transportation industry differs from that of Utilities; this result indicates that the one-digit grouping of industries 40–49 is not an appropriate grouping for the purpose of the overtime analysis. Finally, note that while neither the combinations Retail Trade–Wholesale Trade nor Wholesale Trade–Services can be aggregated together, it appears that the set of coefficients is identical between Retail Trade and the Service industry.

Further comparisons can be made by studying the table. The general conclusion reached from this analysis can, however, be stated simply: it is not a single nonmanufacturing industry's set of coefficients which is causing the hypothesis of equality of coefficients across industries to be rejected.[6] Rather, there appear to be substantial differences among many of the industries.

The Problem of Omitted Variables

In Chapter 5, we argued that to account for the problem of omitted variables, we should allow the intercept term to vary with the establishment size code. The argument basically assumed that large firms have greater flexibility than small firms and can handle rush orders and equipment failures with less recourse to additional overtime. This type of argument may still be relevant for several of the nonmanufacturing industries which in the relevant sense "produce" to order, such as Construction, Transportation, Utilities, and Wholesale Trade. To test this proposition, once again regressions allowing the intercept to vary with establishment size were estimated. These results are reported in Tables 6–5 (the intercepts) and A6–1 (all other coefficients).

As in the manufacturing industries, the coefficients of the explanatory variables (found in appendix Table A6–1) change only marginally from the comparable coefficients in Table 6–3. Unlike the manufacturing results, however, the *F* values do not increase substantially but actually decrease. The cause of this is seen in Table 6–5. Other than in the Transportation

---

[6] This conclusion should be a qualified one, due to the limitations involved in the multiple pairwise Chow test procedure. These limitations are discussed in Chapter 5.

Table 6–5. Intercept Varies with Establishment Size: OLS Estimates of Intercept

Size Class	Construction	Transportation	Mining	Industry Utilities	Wholesale Trade	Retail Trade	Services	Finance
ESC1	-13.312	65.639[a]	-65.777	40.315	109.340	0.896	41.806	59.959-
ESC2	-21.319	40.383	31.803	6.243	125.520	6.289	-64.586[d]	
ESC3	121.290[b,a]	5.844	+7.001	1.216	101.230	-34.803	23.242	13.700
ESC4	46.312	-181.960[d]	60.875	9.635	111.210	-23.202[d]	55.570	27.968
ESC5	46.224	31.937	12.160	5.484	59.490	-8.394	-32.219	78.062
ESC6	37.736	-45.286	7.976	-34.323	99.155	-17.819	9.073	63.825
ESC7	11.495	-36.421	35.087	-20.844	125.560	-73.125	-7.381	6.406
ESC8	160.080	40.470	300.87[d]	-24.502	79.158[d]	-68.692	-31.111	192.870
ESC9		119.050[c]		124.120[a,d]	-61.935	-101.460		-112.680

[a] Coefficient statistically significantly different from zero at 0.90 level of significance; two-tailed test.
[b] Coefficient statistically significantly different from zero at 0.95 level of significance; two-tailed test.
[c] Coefficient statistically significantly different from zero at 0.99 level of significance; two-tailed test.
[d] Coefficient is intercept value for that size class. All other coefficients are deviations from this coefficient.
ESC values: (1) 1–25, (2) 25–50, (3) 50–100, (4) 100–250, (5) 250–500, (6) 500–1000, (7) 1000–2500, (8) and (9) greater than 2500 employees.

industry, the constant terms do not appear to vary significantly across size classes. Furthermore, ignoring the statistical significance of the intercepts and considering only their point estimates, we again observe no systematic size pattern existing across size classes within industries. The conclusion to be drawn from this analysis is that the disequilibrium components of overtime do not appear to be correlated with establishment size in the nonmanufacturing industries. If the "omitted variables" are uncorrelated with establishment size, the coefficient estimates in Table 6–3 will remain unbiased.

Establishment Size and the Overtime Decision

In addition to allowing the intercept to vary with establishment size class, several reasons were advanced in the previous chapter for allowing the coefficients of the other explanatory variables to vary across size classes of establishments within an industry. These arguments related to indivisibilities inherent in small firms as well as to various technical constraints that may exist in production processes such as integrated assembly line operations, fixed men–machine ratios, etc. that might be related to establishment size. One might expect a priori, however, especially in the Service and Trade industries, that "production processes" are more homogeneous across size classes within a nonmanufacturing industry than they are in the manufacturing industries.

To test whether the structure is constant across establishment size classes, the five nonmanufacturing industries with greater than 100 observations were each divided by establishment size class into the maximum number of subgroups; the results reported in Table A6–2, and summarized in the Tabulation below. Again, within each industry a Chow test was conducted; and *only* for

Industry	F Value	Degrees of Freedom	Action
Construction	4.320	(42,236)	Reject at 0.995 level
Transportation	0.703	(56,190)	Not reject at 0.90 level
Utilities	0.566	(56,121)	Not reject at 0.90 level
Wholesale Trade	0.121	(49,195)	Not reject at 0.90 level
Retail Trade	0.294	(49,116)	Not reject at 0.90 level

the Construction industry could the null hypothesis that the set of coefficients was invariant across different size groups be rejected. This should be contrasted with the manufacturing industry results in which the null hypothesis was rejected in five of eight cases; even when establishments were only divided into three size classes per industry.

It should be cautioned, however, that even if the *RATIO* coefficient differs substantially between subgroups within an industry, the insignificance of most of the other coefficients will bias the test towards not rejecting the hypothesis that the *set* of coefficients are equal. In addition, dividing each industry into seven to nine groups also drastically decreases the degrees of freedom and hence the significance of the *RATIO* coefficient; the coefficient in which we are primarily interested. An alternative is to estimate a single regression within each industry allowing only the *RATIO* coefficient to vary with establishment size while constraining all the other coefficients to be constant within the industry. That is, we again define dummy variables D_j such that

$$D_j = \begin{cases} 1 & \text{if the establishment is in ESC}_j \quad (j = 1, \ldots, 9) \\ 0 & \text{otherwise} \end{cases}$$

Then the equation to be estimated is

$$OT = a_0 + \sum_{j=1}^{9} a_j D_j RATIO + \sum_{j=1}^{5} B_j X_j \tag{6.2}$$

where the X_j are the other explanatory variables. Unlike the corresponding manufacturing industry regressions, the intercept term is not allowed to vary with establishment size here. This was done since the results of Table 6–5 seem to indicate that the intercept does not vary with establishment sizes.[7] This also enables us to avoid the collinearity problem alluded to in the previous chapter.

Equation (6.2) was estimated for the six industry groups in which the *RATIO* coefficient had previously proven significant. The estimated *RATIO* coefficients for each size class are presented in Table 6–6, and the remaining coefficients are relegated to Table A6–3 in the appendix to the chapter. The most striking conclusion to be drawn is that all of the coefficients are positive and almost all statistically significantly different from zero. In addition, although a formal statistical test of the equality of the sets of coefficients within an industry has not been conducted, within each industry most of the coefficients are of the same order of magnitude. Hence any change in the overtime premium could be expected, *ceteris paribus*, to effect all size classes

---

[7] In almost all cases estimates of (2) also had smaller residual variances than estimates of corresponding equations which allowed the intercept to vary with establishment size. These other estimates are not reported here.

Table 6–6. Ratio Coefficient Varies with Establishment Size Code

Size Class	Construction	Transportation	Industry Utilities	Wholesale Trade	Retail Trade	Services
ESC1	20.957[c]	54.814[c]	22.370[c]	32.011[c]	39.031[c]	44.126[c]
ESC2	22.956[c]	49.697[c]	12.786[b]	39.462[c]	39.442[c]	30.715[c]
ESC3	22.247[c]	42.923[a]	11.686[b]	29.355[b]	29.588[c]	40.029[c]
ESC4	42.981[c]	42.034[c]	14.066[b]	34.651[c]	34.325[c]	39.842[b]
ESC5	43.339[c]	47.272[c]	13.079[b]	27.726[b]	34.783[b]	21.346[a]
ESC6	36.087[c]	37.037[c]	7.220	33.922[c]	30.705[b]	32.498[b]
ESC7	34.448[b]	36.856[c]	8.921[b]	33.242[b]	19.374	27.943[a]
ESC8	70.141[a]	48.900[c]	8.669[b]		18.567	26.314
ESC9		26.009[c]	11.919[b]	14.111	8.325	

[a] Coefficient statistically significantly different from zero at 0.90 level of significance; two-tailed test.
[b] Coefficient statistically significantly different from zero at 0.95 level of significance; two-tailed test.
[c] Coefficient statistically significantly different from zero at 0.99 level of significance; two-tailed test.

of firms within an industry quite uniformly for these nonmanufacturing industries.

These results are in sharp contrast to those from the analogous experiment for the manufacturing industries. In the manufacturing industries, there was no consistent pattern of sign or significance of the corresponding coefficients, either within or across industries. The implication is that either: (1) each one of these nonmanufacturing industries is more homogeneous than any of the manufacturing industries (i.e., within an industry group, establishments of different sizes appear to have similar "production processes") or (2) the sample sizes in the manufacturing industries were not large enough to conduct a meaningful analysis; and if a larger sample was available, each manufacturing industry might also turn out to be "homogeneous." Knowledge of which of these explanations is true would obviously influence decisions concerning the wisdom of increasing the overtime premium to reduce overtime in manufacturing industries. Given the available data, however, it is impossible to decide which of the two explanations is correct.

The Effect of Unions

We argued in the previous chapter that the total effect of unions on overtime could be separated into at least three parts: Union rules calling for overtime pay for weekend or holiday work may cause unionized firms to have different intercepts than nonunionized firms. Unions may affect the levels of the other explanatory variables, such as the relative wage rate or the amount of paid sick leave received. Finally, unions may alter the underlying employment–hours trade-off through rules concerning layoffs, stand-by crews, etc. While the first two effects are captured in equation (6.1), the latter is not. To test for such structural differences, the manufacturing industries were each divided into two subgroups depending upon whether the majority of the establishments' production workers were covered by collective bargaining agreements. Separate regressions were estimated for each group, and in all cases the hypothesis that the set of coefficients was the same for both groups (unions do not effect the underlying structural relationship) could not be rejected.

This procedure was repeated for the nonmanufacturing industry groups. The regression results are reported in Table A6–4 in the appendix to the chapter. The similarity of the coefficients for the two classes of establishments within an industry is most striking and indeed a Chow test indicates that the hypothesis of the equality of the set of coefficients for both groups within an industry *cannot* be rejected.[8] Similar to the results reported in the previous chapter, unions do not appear to affect the underlying structural relationship between overtime and the explanatory variables in the nonmanufacturing industries.

Component Industries and Overtime Behavior

As in the previous chapter, the final question to be considered here is the legitimacy of aggregating the two-digit nonmanufacturing industries into the larger groups used in this study. Establishments in different component two-digit industries within one of these groups may have vastly different technical processes of operation. For example, Retail Trade includes both Department Stores (S.I.C. 53) and Automobile Service Stations (S.I.C. 55). Since the relationship between overtime and the explanatory variables is expected to be invariant only across establishments using similar production processes, we might therefore believe that disaggregation is necessary.

Those nonmanufacturing industries that had a sufficient number of observations for the basic regression, equation (6.1), to be estimated for each component two-digit industry were selected.[9] These regressions were run and the results reported in Table A6.5 in the appendix to the chapter. Again Chow tests were conducted and in three of the four cases the null hypothesis that the set of coefficients was identical across two-digit industries in the same group was *rejected* at the 95 percent level of significance.

Industry	F Value	Degrees of Freedom	Action
Construction	2.585	(14,264)	Reject at 95% level
Transportation	2.859	(7,224)	Reject at 95% level
Utilities	1.216	(7,170)	Not reject at 90% level
Retail Trade	11.988	(42,123)	Reject at 95% level

Only in the Utilities industry (Communications S.I.C. 48, Electric, Gas, and Sanitary Systems S.I.C. 49) could the null hypothesis not be rejected. For the

---

[8] The following values of the relevant F ratio (with corresponding degrees of freedom) were all too low to reject the null hypothesis of equality of the sets of coefficients at the 90 percent level.

Mining	$F = 0.626 \, (6, 25)$	Wholesale Trade	$F = 0.919 \, (6, 232)$
Construction	$F = 0.263 \, (6, 272)$	Retail Trade	$F = 1.153 \, (6, 160)$
Transportation	$F = 0.528 \, (6, 227)$	Services	$F = 0.605 \, (6, 77)$
Utilities	$F = 0.904 \, (6, 172)$		

[9] These were the Construction, Transportation, Utilities, and Retail Trade groups.

other groups, disaggregation appears to be necessary. The results for Retail Trade are interesting in particular, since in a different context, Cotterill [19] found that it was inappropriate to aggregate the Retail Trade industries together when estimating demand for labor (measured in " quality-corrected " number of employees) equations.[10]

Summary

The important results found in this chapter can be summarized briefly.

As in the manufacturing industries, observed overtime hours per man has been shown to be significantly positively related to the ratio of weekly fixed employment costs per employee to the overtime wage rate in the majority (six of eight) of the nonmanufacturing industry groups. Once again the relationship between overtime per man and the set of explanatory variables is not uniform across all these industry groups.

Within a given group, however, the relationship between overtime and *RATIO* appears to be invariant across establishments of different size classes. This result is in sharp contrast to that found in the manufacturing industries and may imply one of two things: either that different size classes of establishments are more homogeneous within a nonmanufacturing than manufacturing industry, or that within each manufacturing industry the number of observations in each size class was too small to make meaningful comparisons across size classes. Without additional information, it is impossible for us to reject either of these explanations.

Within a major industry group, unions do not appear to alter the underlying structural relationship between overtime and the explanatory variables. However, different component industries within such groups often exhibit significantly different relationships between overtime and the explanatory variables. Both these conclusions are identical to those obtained from the analogous experiments for the manufacturing industries. On the other hand, the disequilibrium components of overtime do not appear to vary substantially within an industry with establishment size. This is in contrast to the manufacturing industries, in which establishment size did appear to be related to the level of disequilibrium overtime, although the relationship was not constant across industries.

Finally, in the Construction and Wholesale Trade industries, an extremely

---

[10] Cotterill's study utilized aggregated cross-section census data with the mean value of the variables within an SMSA as the units of observation and ignored the overtime–employment trade-off.

strong negative relationship between the establishment wage rate and the amount of overtime is present. This may be caused by employers considering the three-way trade-off among the wage rate they offer, the quality of labor they attract, and consequently the amount of overtime required to achieve a desired level of labor services.

7

Conclusions and Implications for Manpower Policy

The primary goal of this study has been to empirically test the hypothesis that high quasi-fixed supplementary labor compensation costs per man relative to the overtime wage rate tend to induce a substitution of overtime hours for employment. To provide a framework for testing this hypothesis, several models of the firm's short-run employment-hours decisions were presented in Chapters 2 and 3. Among the conclusions reached in these chapters was a refutation of the common notion that a stochastic absentee rate will always lead to an increase in overtime above the level that would prevail in a certainty-equivalent absentee rate case. A justification was provided for the familiar phenomenon that not all employees of a given firm work the same number of hours. The empirically testable conditions under which it would be rational for management to agree to union demands that overtime be assigned on the basis of seniority were indicated. We also explicitly indicated how cross-section regressions seeking to explain interfirm variations in overtime hours per man will be affected by firms being in short-run equilibrium along the dynamic adjustment paths derived from the models, rather than all being in stationary equilibrium.

These models were used as the basis for our empirical analysis presented in Chapters 5 and 6, in which we attempted to explain intraindustry variations in observed overtime hours per man using individual establishment cross-section data. These data were derived from unpublished compilations provided to us from the Bureau of Labor Statistics' survey of "Employer Expenditures for Selected Compensation Practices, 1966." The results of our analysis have been discussed in the summaries to these chapters and need not be repeated in detail here. What most strikingly emerges, however, is a confirmation of our principal hypothesis; in the vast majority of both the manufacturing and nonmanufacturing industries the observed annual over-time hours per man are significantly positively related to the ratio of weekly fixed labor costs per man to the overtime premium wage.

The existence of a significant qualitative relationship does not in itself provide us with sufficient information to make any policy recommendations. What we require are quantitative estimates of the magnitude of the relationship. Fortunately, such information can be obtained almost directly from our estimated regression coefficients and we can consequently attempt to answer the question, "What would the effect of an increase in the overtime premium be, *ceteris paribus*, on the level of employment and the number of overtime hours worked per man?"

For the sixteen manufacturing industries analyzed in our study, Table 7–1 contains the required information. The first column in this table presents the estimated values of the coefficients of the *RATIO* variable obtained for our basic model.[1] The next two columns list the mean values of *RATIO* and observed annual overtime hours per man within an industry, as calculated by us for the establishments in our sample. The estimated elasticity of annual overtime per man with respect to *RATIO*, evaluated at the means of both variables, is found in column 4. These elasticities indicate the percentage change in annual overtime per man that would result, on average, from a 1 percent change in *RATIO*. Since the denominator of *RATIO* is equal to the overtime wage rate, the elasticity of overtime with respect to the overtime premium can then be directly calculated.

More interesting than the elasticity estimates, however, is the effect of a given discrete change in the overtime premium on overtime and employment. In particular, previously proposed congressional bills suggested increasing the overtime premium wage from one-and-a-half to twice the straight-time hourly wage and we will consider the effects of such a change here.[2] An increase in the overtime premium of this magnitude would cause a decrease in *RATIO* of 25 percent. Therefore multiplying the coefficient of *RATIO* (column 1) by 0.25 times the mean value of *RATIO* (column 2) yields the average decrease in annual overtime per man for each industry. These estimates are presented in column 5, and we note that the average decrease in overtime per man would vary between approximately 5 and 120 hours per year. Dividing these figures by the corresponding mean value of overtime per man in the industry generates the corresponding mean percentage decreases in overtime per man, which are found in column 6. For over three-quarters of these industries, the estimated percentage reduction is greater than 10 percent. A substantial portion of the overtime hours that are being worked would be eliminated by this increase in the overtime premium. It is especially interesting to note the estimated percentage decrease of almost 40 percent in the Paper industry (S.I.C. 26). Segments of this industry have continuous-process operations and management has argued that this "technical constraint" was the primary

---

[1] These coefficients are found in the regressions reported in Table 5–1.

[2] See the *Overtime Pay Penalty Act of 1964* [70].

Table 7-1. Overtime and Employment Changes Resulting from a Change in the Overtime Premium

$$OT = \alpha_0 + \alpha_1 RATIO + \alpha_2 STD.HRS + \alpha_3 WAGE + \alpha_4 NEWSEN + \alpha_5 ABSEN + \alpha_6 UNION$$

Industry	S.I.C. Code	(1)	(2)	(3)	(4)	(5)	(6)	(7)
Food	20	26.398	5.215	183.740	0.749	34.416	18.731	1.721
Textile	22	29.898	3.918	194.395	0.602	29.285	15.065	1.464
Apparel	23	5.137	4.843	69.883	0.356	6.220	8.900	0.311
Lumber	24	9.876	4.351	210.300	0.204	10.743	5.108	0.537*
Furniture	25	21.930	4.056	149.523	0.637	22.237	14.872	1.112*
Paper	26	85.758	5.737	309.199	1.591	122.998	39.780	6.150
Printing	27	25.793	4.592	153.720	0.796	29.610	19.263	1.481
Chemicals	28	25.805	6.190	194.040	0.823	39.933	20.580	1.997
Rubber	30	40.429	5.446	221.510	0.993	55.044	24.849	2.752
Stone, clay, glass	32	11.029	6.099	215.977	0.247	16.816	7.786	0.841*
Primary Metal	33	19.727	5.564	221.287	0.496	27.440	12.400	1.372
Fabricated Metal	34	26.392	5.626	209.055	0.710	37.120	17.756	1.856
Machinery	35	33.695	5.764	271.339	0.715	48.554	17.894	2.428
Electrical equipment	36	32.481	5.443	151.023	1.170	44.199	29.266	2.210
Transportation equipment	37	4.121	4.495	214.195	0.086	4.631	2.162	0.232*
Misc. Manufacturing	39	53.146	5.245	159.735	1.745	69.688	43.627	3.484

* Regression coefficient on which calculations were based was not statistically significantly different from zero at 0.95 level of significance.
Column 1: Coefficient of RATIO variable in regression.
Column 2: Mean value of RATIO in industry for establishments in the sample.
Column 3: Mean value of annual overtime per man for establishments in the sample.
Column 4: Elasticity of annual overtime per man with respect to RATIO.
Column 5: Estimated decrease in annual overtime per man when overtime premium increased to double time.
Column 6: Corresponding estimated percentage change in overtime per man.
Column 7: Corresponding estimated percentage change in employment, assuming total man-hours remain constant.

cause of overtime in the industry.[3] It appears, however, that conscious marginal decisions, not the technology, are responsible for much of the overtime worked in the industry.

If we adhere to our *ceteris paribus* assumptions and postulate that total man-hours demanded by each establishment would then remain constant after an increase in the overtime premium, then *upper limits* to the estimated increases in employment that would result can be obtained.[4] Assuming that the decreases in overtime could all be translated into new full-time employees, each working 2,000 hours per year, the percentage increase in employment would be given by (change in annual overtime per man/2000) × 100. These estimates are presented in column 7. Again, the estimates are remarkably stable, in the majority of these industries the magnitude is in the order of 1 to 3 percent. In fact, applying these estimates to the actual industry production-worker employment figures found in *Employment and Earning Statistics* [77] for 1966, indicates an overall percentage increase in employment for these sixteen industries in the order of 1.6 percent. These industries had an average production-worker employment level of approximately 13,616,000 in 1966 and the overall increase in the number of full-time positions would have been about 218,500. Naturally, if the decreases in overtime were translated instead into increases in part-time employment, this latter figure would be larger.

Table 7–2 contains a second set of estimates for the manufacturing industries. The *RATIO* coefficients presented in column 1 of this table are obtained from the regressions in which the intercept term was allowed to vary with establishment size, in order to capture the varying disequilibrium component of overtime.[5] The estimated changes in overtime and employment found in columns 5, 6 and 7 are of the same order of magnitude as those in the previous table. Finally, Table 7–3 presents the analogous results for the nonmanufacturing industries to those found in Table 7–1.[6] These results cannot be generalized to the whole population of nonmanufacturing establishments because only those establishments that had positive levels of overtime

---

[3] See [70]. The argument given is that the 168 hour workweek is split up into four approximately equal-size shifts of 40, 40, 40, and 48 hours a week. On average then, each employee works at least two hours overtime per week. However, the technology does not require this. An alternative would be to have four shifts of 40 hours and only a skeleton maintenance staff keeping the process going during the remaining eight hours per week. This scheme would of course require an increase in employment to achieve the the same level of output. Management may therefore be consciously trading-off overtime and additional employment.

[4] This assumption will be discussed in detail below.

[5] These results are found in Table A5–1.

[6] The *RATIO* coefficients are derived from Table 6–3. Similar estimates to those found in Table 7–2 are not presented for the nonmanufacturing industries since the intercept terms did not appear to vary appreciably with establishment size there.

Table 7-2. Overtime and Employment Changes Resulting from a Change in the Overtime Premium

$$OT = \sum_{j=1}^{9} b_{0j}ESC_j + b_1RATIO + b_2STD.HRS + b_3WAGE + b_4NEWSEN + b_5ABSEN + b_6UNION$$

Industry	S.I.C. Code	(1)	(2)	(3)	(4)	(5)	(6)	(7)
Food	20	23.307	5.215	183.740	0.661	30.387	16.538	1.519
Textile	22	36.294	3.918	194.395	0.731	35.550	18.287	1.777
Apparel	23	5.063	4.843	69.883	0.350	6.130	8.772	0.307
Lumber	24	20.673	4.351	210.300	0.427	22.487	10.693	1.124*
Furniture	25	39.848	4.056	149.523	1.157	40.406	27.023	2.020*
Paper	26	80.663	5.737	309.199	1.496	115.691	37.416	5.785
Printing	27	27.557	4.592	153.720	0.823	31.635	20.580	1.582
Chemicals	28	24.573	6.190	194.040	0.784	38.027	19.597	1.901
Rubber	30	50.747	5.446	221.510	1.247	69.092	31.191	3.455
Stone, clay, glass	32	9.297	6.099	215.977	0.208	14.176	6.563	0.709*
Primary Metal	33	25.628	5.564	221.287	0.652	35.649	16.110	1.782
Fabricated Metal	34	25.964	5.626	209.055	0.698	36.518	17.468	1.826
Machinery	35	33.696	5.764	271.339	0.715	48.556	17.895	2.428
Electrical equipment	36	33.967	5.443	151.023	1.224	46.221	30.605	2.311
Transportation equipment	37	-1.972	4.495	214.195	-0.041	-2.216	-1.035	-0.111*
Misc. Manufacturing	39	70.611	5.245	159.735	2.318	92.589	57.964	4.629

* Regression coefficient on which calculations were based was not statistically significantly different from zero at 0.95 level of significance.
Column 1: Coefficient of RATIO variable in regression.
Column 2: Mean value of RATIO in industry for establishments in the sample.
Column 3: Mean value of annual overtime per man for establishments in the sample.
Column 4: Elasticity of annual overtime per man with respect to RATIO.
Column 5: Estimated decrease in annual overtime per man when overtime premium increased to double time.
Column 6: Corresponding estimated percentage change in overtime per man.
Column 7: Corresponding estimated percentage change in employment, assuming total man-hours remain constant.

Table 7-3. Overtime and Employment Changes Resulting from a Change in the Overtime Premium

$$OT = \alpha_0 + \alpha_1 RATIO + \alpha_2 STD.HRS + \alpha_3 WAGE + \alpha_4 NEWSEN + \alpha_5 ABSEN + \alpha_6 UNION$$

Industry	S.I.C. Code	(1)	(2)	(3)	(4)	(5)	(6)	(7)
Mining	10–14	0.343	6.644	151.827	0.014	0.570	0.375	0.028*
Construction	15–17	30.929	3.331	125.217	0.822	25.756	20.569	1.288
Transportation	40–42	42.888	5.734	186.645	1.317	60.058	32.179	3.003
Utilities	48, 49	7.899	6.988	121.731	0.454	13.782	11.322	0.689
Wholesale Trade	50	39.093	5.110	188.992	1.057	49.941	26.425	2.497
Retail trade	52–59	35.101	3.911	110.051	1.247	35.022	31.823	1.751
Services	70–89	40.370	3.958	89.819	1.779	39.946	44.474	1.997
Financial	60–66	14.673	5.997	122.222	0.719	21.998	17.999	1.100*

* Regression coefficient on which calculations were based was not statistically significantly different from zero at 0.95 level of significance.
Column 1: Coefficient of RATIO variable in the regression.
Column 2: Mean value of RATIO in industry for establishments in the sample.
Column 3: Mean value of annual overtime per man for establishments in the sample.
Column 4: Elasticity of annual overtime per man with respect to RATIO.
Column 5: Estimated decrease in annual overtime per man when overtime premium increased to double time.
Column 6: Corresponding estimated percentage change in overtime per man.
Column 7: Corresponding estimated percentage change in employment, assuming total man-hours remain constant.

were included as observations in the nonmanufacturing regressions. Nevertheless, the estimated average percentage increase in employment for establishments in the sample, caused by an increase in the overtime premium wage to twice the straight-time wage, is again in the order 1 to 3 percent for the majority of the nonmanufacturing industries.

At first glance then, the implications of our study for manpower policy seems obvious. An increase in the overtime premium from time-and-a-half to double-time would appear to have a significant impact on reducing unemployment. However, even if we ignore the obvious inflationary impact of such a move, this implication must be qualified by three important sets of factors; the relevance of our *ceteris paribus* assumptions, supply-side considerations, and our empirical results when data for a given two-digit industry was segmented into smaller subgroups. Each set of qualifications will be discussed in turn.

Our *ceteris paribus* assumption that total man-hours demanded by employers would remain constant if the overtime premium was increased and consequently that the resulting decrease in overtime could all be translated into increased employment is probably not valid. To verify this assumption would require a fairly complete econometric model in which the effects of increased labor costs on prices, product demand, and capital–labor trade-offs were taken into account. An increase in the overtime premium would have both a scale effect and two sets of substitution effects. We have taken account in our calculations only of the substitution of employment for overtime. On the other hand, a substitution of capital for both overtime and employment (i.e., labor-saving equipment) may occur since labor services would become relatively more expensive than capital. Similarly, if an increase in the overtime premium resulted in an increase in the final product's price and a consequent decrease in the quantity demanded of the product, then there would be a scale effect reducing the demand for labor services.[7] In sum, while our estimates of the changes in overtime may be fairly accurate, our estimates of the resulting employment changes must be regarded only as upper bounds.

We have also neglected throughout our discussion any supply-side considerations. An increase in the overtime premium might, depending upon the relative strengths of employees' income and substitution effects, increase employees' demand for overtime. This effect could be eliminated if the income from an increase in the overtime premium were placed in a "social welfare fund" rather than being given to the individual workers.[8] Supply-side

---

[7] We have shown in the appendix to Chapter 2 that under certain conditions a decrease in scale would affect only the equilibrium level of employment, not the equilibrium level of hours per man. The negative inflationary effects of the proposal are obvious and need no further explanation.

[8] See [71], p. 48.

considerations may also be important, however, if the resulting decrease in overtime per man causes increased moonlighting by currently employed workers seeking to maintain their income levels. While moonlighters are unlikely to seek full-time jobs, if the increase in employment opportunities caused by an increase in the overtime premium results in primarily part-time employment vacancies, then they may absorb a number of these positions. Consequently, our estimate of the reduction in unemployment that would occur should be reduced even further.

Finally, the results of our empirical analyses in which the coefficient of the *RATIO* variable was allowed to vary across component industries and size classes of establishments within a given industry group should be reconsidered. In both the manufacturing and the nonmanufacturing industries, this coefficient appeared to vary significantly across component industries. Hence, the effect of an increase in the overtime premium would not be uniform, even across three-digit industries within a given two-digit manufacturing industry.

The relationship between establishment size and the size and significance of the *RATIO* coefficient is of particular interest since many have argued that there are indivisibilities inherent in small establishments that may prevent them from making the relevant marginal decisions.[9] If this were true, we would expect small-size establishments to exhibit small and insignificant *RATIO* coefficients. Others have argued that technical constraints in production processes such as assembly-line crews and fixed men–machine ratios prevent changes in the quasi-fixed costs per man from influencing the overtime–employment decisions. For size classes of establishments which face such constraints, we would again expect to observe small insignificant *RATIO* coefficients. Unless the relationship between overtime per man and *RATIO* is fairly stable across size classes of establishments, however, it is unlikely that an increase in the overtime premium could be considered as a feasible policy alternative.

Our empirical results are somewhat intriguing. For the nonmanufacturing industries, the *RATIO* coefficient was positive, statistically significant, and uniformly tolerably stable with an industry across almost all size classes of establishments. However, the results for the manufacturing industries are quite different. The coefficients appear to vary in magnitude across size classes of establishments within an industry. Moreover, there exists no consistent pattern of which *RATIO* coefficients are positive and statistically significant, either within or across industries. Indeed in several cases, it is the smallest size class of establishments that has the largest and most significant coefficient.

---

[9] See *Overtime Pay Penalty Act of 1964* [70].

The implication that one draws is that either different size classes of establishments are more homogeneous within a nonmanufacturing than manufacturing industry, or that the number of observations in each size class was too small to make meaningful comparisons using the manufacturing industry data.[10] That is, while it is reasonable to assume that technical constraints in the production processes may be prevalent in certain size classes of establishments within each manufacturing industry, it is also conceivable that the insignificant coefficients are caused by the relatively smaller sample sizes for the manufacturing than nonmanufacturing industries. Without additional data, we cannot distinguish between these two hypotheses.[11] However, if the former is true, this would tend to even further reduce our estimated decrease in unemployment. An increase in the overtime premium would also cause distribution affects in this case, by effectively discriminating against those firms for which overtime per man is not significantly related to the ratio of quasi-fixed labor costs per man to the overtime premium wage.

Given the above qualifications, our conclusion with respect to manpower policy must be a negative one at this time: Although within the vast majority of both the manufacturing and nonmanufacturing industries, annual overtime hours per man are significantly positively related to the ratio of weekly fixed supplementary labor costs per man to the overtime wage premium, it does *not* appear that increasing the overtime premium would be an effective method of decreasing unemployment at this time. If further research indicates that the relationship is fairly uniform across size classes of establishments within each manufacturing industry, however, we would be more disposed to recommend such an action to decrease unemployment during a future noninflationary period.

---

[10] The average sample size for the manufacturing industries was 60 establishments as compared to over 150 establishments in each nonmanufacturing industry group.

[11] The B.L.S. conducted a survey similar to the one used in this study in 1968. This survey is currently being processed and may in the future provided the additional body of data necessary to ascertain the relationship between the *RATIO* coefficient and establishment size in the manufacturing industries as well as to test for the stability of the *RATIO* coefficient for each industry over time.

Appendixes

Appendix to Chapter 2

Conditions (2.3a), (2.3b), and (2.3c) in the text implicitly determine M^* and H^* as functions of all of the parameters in the model. Totally differentiating each of these necessary conditions and then solving using Cramer's rule, we can obtain explicit expressions for the partial derivatives of the equilibrium values M^* and H^* with respect to all of the parameters in the model.

Denote by Δ the expression,

$$\lambda[(2F_1F_2F_{12} - F_1^2F_{22} - F_2^2F_{11}) - 2F_1F_2^2/M] \tag{A2.1}$$

The expression in the brackets is that found in necessary condition (2.2b) from the text and is positive. The Lagrangian multiplier λ has the interpretation of the negative of marginal cost and from conditions (2.2a) and (2.3b) must be negative. Consequently Δ is negative. Then following the procedure suggested in the first paragraph yields, after simplification,

$$\frac{\partial H}{\partial w_0} = -\frac{F_1F_2}{\Delta} > 0 \quad \text{where } w_0 = w_1 + (r+q)T \tag{A2.2a}$$

$$\frac{\partial H}{\partial \overline{H}} = [(1-b)w_2]\frac{\partial H}{\partial w_0} < 0 \tag{A2.2b}$$

$$\frac{\partial H}{\partial w_2} = \frac{-w_0F_1b}{\Delta\lambda} < 0 \tag{A2.2c}$$

$$\frac{\partial H}{\partial b} = \frac{-(w_2F_1M)(w_0 + w_2\overline{H})}{(\Delta\lambda)} < 0 \tag{A2.2d}$$

Conditions (2.2a) and (2.3c) immediately imply that

$$\frac{\partial M}{\partial w_0} < 0 \qquad \frac{\partial M}{\partial \overline{H}}, \frac{\partial M}{\partial w_2}, \frac{\partial M}{\partial_b} > 0 \tag{A2.2e}$$

We argued in the text that a result intuitively plausible to us was that equilibrium hours should be invariant to scale. However, the above procedure yields that

$$\frac{\partial H}{\partial L} = \frac{F_1(w_2b + \lambda F_{12}) - \lambda F_{11}F_2}{\Delta} \tag{A2.3}$$

113

For equilibrium hours to be invariant to scale, the numerator of this expression must be equal to zero. Substituting for $w_2 b$ from (2.3b) in the text indicates that we require

$$M = \frac{F_1 F_2}{F_1 F_{12} - F_2 F_{11}} \qquad (A2.4)$$

Without further restrictions, it has proven impossible to determine the whole class of functions which satisfies equation (A2.4). It is easy to check however that the Cobb–Douglas function satisfies the condition while the CES labor-input function does not, for elasticities of substitutions different from unity. This may lead one to conjecture that the Cobb–Douglas function is the only function that satisfies the condition and consequently that our invariance assumption is overly restrictive. To see that this is not the case, consider the special case of the multiplicatively separable version of equation (2.2).

$$L = f(M)g(H)$$

For this particular case, condition (A2.4) becomes

$$M = \frac{ff'}{f'^2 - ff''} \qquad (A2.5)$$

This can be rewritten as $f'' - (f'^2/f) - (f'/M) = 0$, which is a special case of Liouville's equation;[1] and, after manipulation, it can be shown to be equivalent to

$$\frac{d}{dM}\left[\log \frac{f(M)}{f'(M)}\right] = \frac{1}{M} \qquad (A2.6)$$

Integrating both sides with respect to M and taking exponents, we obtain

$$\frac{f(M)}{f'(M)} = \frac{M}{c}, \qquad c \text{ a constant} \qquad (A2.7)$$

This can be rewritten as

$$\frac{d}{dM}[\log f(M)] = \frac{c}{M} \qquad (A2.7a)$$

---

[1] See Murphy [49], p. 385.

Consequently, integrating and simplifying yields

$$f(M) = c_1 M^c, \qquad c_1 \text{ a constant} \qquad \text{(A2.8)}$$

Crucially then, the class of labor-input functions that are multiplicatively separable in M and H for which equilibrium hours are invariant to scale, can be written

$$L = c_1 M^c g(H), \qquad c, c_1 \text{ both constants} \qquad \text{(A2.9)}$$

We recall from Chapter 3 that if we assume that labor is homogeneous and that the marginal contribution to labor services of an additional hour of work by one employee is independent of the hours of work of all other employees, then the labor-input function can be written as $L = Mg(H)$. This is a special case of equation (A2.9) and hence the assumption of invariance of equilibrium hours to scale is not as restrictive as one would initially expect.

Note, in conclusion, that this assumption immediately implies from equations (2.2a) and (2.3c) that

$$\frac{\partial M^*}{\partial L} > 0 \qquad \text{(A2.10)}$$

Appendix to Chapter 3

The Model

The comparative static results of this section are derived by using Cramer's rule. Utilizing the sign pattern of D_{ij}, the following results are obtained. In cases where partials are ambiguous, it proved impossible to assign them definite signs when the explicit values of D_{ij} were substituted in. To avoid unnecessary detail we eliminate listing the values of D_{ij} here; they can be explicitly calculated from the text.

Labor Services

$$\frac{\partial M_1}{\partial L} = \frac{D_{21}}{D} > 0, \qquad \frac{\partial H_1}{\partial L} = \frac{D_{22}}{D} = 0, \qquad \frac{\partial \theta}{\partial L} = \frac{D_{25}}{D} = 0$$

$$\frac{\partial M_2}{\partial L} = \frac{D_{23}}{D} > 0, \qquad \frac{\partial H_2}{\partial L} = \frac{D_{24}}{D} = 0$$

Interest Rate

$$\frac{\partial M_1}{\partial r} = -c'(\theta) \frac{D_{51}}{D} = ?\dagger, \qquad \frac{\partial H_1}{\partial r} = -c'(\theta) \frac{D_{52}}{D} > 0, \qquad \frac{\partial \theta}{\partial r} = -c'(\theta) \frac{D_{55}}{D} < 0$$

$$\frac{\partial M_2}{\partial r} = -c'(\theta) \frac{D_{53}}{D} < 0, \qquad \frac{\partial H_2}{\partial r} = -c'(\theta) \frac{D_{54}}{D} > 0$$

Productivity

$$\frac{\partial M_1}{\partial K} = -M_2 \beta(H_2) \frac{\partial M_1}{\partial L} + \gamma_2 \beta'(H_2) \frac{D_{31}}{D} < 0, \qquad \frac{\partial H_1}{\partial K} = \gamma_2 \beta'(H_2) \frac{D_{32}}{D} < 0,$$

$$\frac{\partial \theta}{\partial K} = \gamma_2 \beta'(H_2) \frac{D_{35}}{D} > 0$$

$$\frac{\partial M_2}{\partial K} = -M_2 \beta(H_2) \frac{\partial M_2}{\partial L} + \gamma_2 \beta'(H_2) \frac{D_{33}}{D} = ?, \qquad \frac{\partial H_2}{\partial K} = \gamma_2 \beta'(H_2) \frac{D_{34}}{D} > 0$$

$\dagger\ \partial M_1/\partial r,\ \partial M_1/\partial q_2,\ \partial M_1/\partial w_1 < 0$ if $\gamma_2 K < 1$.

Senior Workers Quit Rate

$$\frac{\partial M_1}{\partial q_2} = M_2 \frac{D_{11}}{D} + \frac{\partial M_1}{\partial r} = ?\dagger, \qquad \frac{\partial H_1}{\partial q_2} = \frac{\partial H_1}{\partial r} > 0, \qquad \frac{\partial \theta}{\partial q_2} = \frac{\partial \theta}{\partial r} < 0$$

$$\frac{\partial M_2}{\partial q_2} = M_2 \frac{D_{13}}{D} + \frac{\partial M_2}{\partial r} < 0, \qquad \frac{\partial H_2}{\partial q_2} = \frac{\partial H_2}{\partial r} > 0$$

Fixed Costs

$$\frac{\partial M_1}{\partial w_1} = \frac{1}{c'} \frac{\partial M_1}{\partial r} - \gamma_1 \frac{D_{41}}{D} = ?\dagger, \qquad \frac{\partial H_1}{\partial w_1} = \frac{1}{c'} \frac{\partial H_1}{\partial r} - \gamma_1 \frac{D_{42}}{D} > 0,$$

$$\frac{\partial \theta}{\partial w_1} = \frac{1}{c'} \frac{\partial \theta}{\partial r} - \gamma_1 \frac{D_{45}}{D} = ?$$

$$\frac{\partial M_2}{\partial w_1} = \frac{1}{c'} \frac{\partial M_2}{\partial r} - \gamma_1 \frac{D_{43}}{D} = ?, \qquad \frac{\partial H_2}{\partial w_1} = \frac{1}{c'} \frac{\partial H_2}{\partial r} - \gamma_1 \frac{D_{44}}{D} > 0$$

Wage Rate

$$\frac{\partial M_1}{\partial w_2} = x_1 \frac{D_{41}}{D} + x_2 \frac{D_{51}}{D} = ?\ddagger, \qquad \frac{\partial H_1}{\partial w_2} = x_1 \frac{D_{42}}{D} + x_2 \frac{D_{52}}{D} < 0,$$

$$\frac{\partial \theta}{\partial w_2} = x_1 \frac{D_{45}}{D} + x_2 \frac{D_{55}}{D} = ?$$

$$\frac{\partial M_2}{\partial w_2} = x_2 \frac{D_{43}}{D} + x_2 \frac{D_{53}}{D} = ?, \qquad \frac{\partial H_2}{\partial w_2} = x_1 \frac{D_{44}}{D} + x_2 \frac{D_{54}}{D} < 0$$

Standard Hours, Overtime Premium

It should be obvious that substituting y_1 or $(b-1)\gamma_2 w_2$ for x_1 and y_2 or $(b-1)w_2$ for x_2 does not effect the sign of the relevant partial. Hence

---

† $\partial M_1/\partial r,\ \partial M_1/\partial q_2,\ \partial M_1/\partial w_1 < 0$ if $\gamma_2 K < 1$.

‡ $\partial M_1/\partial w_2 > 0$ as $\gamma_2 K < 1$.

$$\frac{\partial \text{ variable}}{\partial w_2}, \frac{\partial \text{ variable}}{\partial \bar{H}}, \frac{\partial \text{ variable}}{\partial b}$$

are all of same sign.

Relative Fixed Costs

$$\frac{\partial M_1}{\partial \gamma_1} = -w_1 \frac{D_{41}}{D} < 0, \qquad \frac{\partial H_1}{\partial \gamma_1} = -w_1 \frac{D_{42}}{D} > 0, \qquad \frac{\partial \theta}{\partial \gamma_1} = -w_1 \frac{D_{45}}{D} > 0$$

$$\frac{\partial M_2}{\partial \gamma_1} = -w_1 \frac{D_{43}}{D} = ?, \qquad \frac{\partial H_2}{\partial \gamma_1} = -w_1 \frac{D_{44}}{D} > 0$$

Relative Wage Rate

$$\frac{\partial M_1}{\partial \gamma_2} = K\beta'(H_2) \frac{D_{31}}{D} + x_1 \frac{w_2}{\gamma_2} \frac{D_{41}}{D} = ?, \qquad \frac{\partial H_1}{\partial \gamma_2}$$

$$= K\beta'(H_2) \frac{D_{32}}{D} + x_1 \frac{w_2}{\gamma_2} \frac{D_{42}}{D} < 0$$

$$\frac{\partial M_2}{\partial \gamma_2} = K\beta'(H_2) \frac{D_{33}}{D} + x_1 \frac{w_2}{\gamma_2} \frac{D_{43}}{D} = ?, \qquad \frac{\partial H_2}{\partial \gamma_2}$$

$$= K\beta'(H_2) \frac{D_{34}}{D} + x_1 \frac{w_2}{\gamma_2} \frac{D_{44}}{D} = ?$$

$$\frac{\partial \theta}{\partial \gamma_2} = K\beta'(H_2) \frac{D_{35}}{D} + x_1 \frac{w_2}{\gamma_2} \frac{D_{45}}{D} = ?$$

Dynamics

Since the explicit values of the determinants E and E_{1j} are crucial for the results of this section, we list them here for the interested reader.

$$E = \frac{-\beta(H_1) w_2 \, b \gamma_2 \, \beta(H_1) \beta''(H_1) \gamma_2 \, K\beta''(H_2) c''}{[\beta'(H_1)]^2} < 0$$

$$E_{11} = E < 0, \qquad E_{12} = E_{13} = E_{14} = E_{15} = E_{21} = E_{22} = E_{23} = E_{24} = 0$$

$$E_{25} = \frac{\beta(H_2)[\beta'(H_1)]^2 E}{\beta(H_1)[\beta'(H_2)]^2} < 0, \qquad E_{31} = \frac{\theta}{\beta(H_1)} E < 0, \quad E_{32} = \frac{E}{\beta(H_1)} < 0$$

$$E_{33} = E_{34} = E_{35} = 0, \qquad E_{51} = \theta c''[M_1 \gamma_2 K \beta'(H_1)\beta''(H_2)$$
$$+ K M_2 \beta''(H_1)\beta'(H_2)] < 0$$

$$E_{52} = \frac{E_{51}}{\theta} < 0, \qquad E_{53} = - c''\beta(H_1)\gamma_2 K \beta''(H_2) > 0$$

$$E_{54} = -c''\beta(H_1)\beta''(H_1) > 0, \qquad E_{55} = \frac{- w_2 b\beta(H_1)\beta''(H_1)\beta(H_2)\beta''(H_2)}{[\beta'(H_2)]^2} < 0$$

Appendix to Chapter 4

The data from the B.L.S. survey of "Employer Expenditures for Selected Compensation Practices, 1966" were sent to us in the format found in Table A4–1. As indicated, each establishment record contained observations on up to 62 variables, with each variable being a 9-digit number. Only the data for production workers in the manufacturing industries or nonsupervisory

Table A4–1. B.L.S. Survey Data

Word Number	Description of Data
0 (0–3)	For B.L.S. use only
0 (4–9)	Schedule number
1	Not used
2 (0–3)	SIC code (1)
(4)	Employee group code (2)
(5)	Region code (3)
(6)	Establishment size code (4)
(7)	Met–nonmet code (5)
(8)	Union–nonunion code (6)
(9)	For B.L.S. use only
	Digit 9 of the remaining words are for B.L.S. use
3 (0–8)	Number of employees
4 (0–8)	Gross payroll
5 (0–8)	Total man-hours
6 (0–8)	Vacation expenditure
7 (0–8)	Holiday expenditure
8 (0–8)	Sick leave expenditure
9 (0–8)	Civic and other leave expenditure rates
10 (0–8)	Overtime payments at straight-time
11 (0–8)	Overtime payments at premium rates
12 (0–8)	Shift premiums
13 (0 -8)	Nonproduction bonuses
14 (0–8)	Terminal payments
15 (0–8)	Life insurance expenditures
16 (0–8)	Health insurance expenditures
17 (0–8)	Pension and retirement expenditures
18 (0–8)	Payments to vacation and holiday funds
19 (0–8)	Payments to severance and SUB funds
20 (0–8)	Payments to savings and thrift plans
21 (0–8)	Payments to other private welfare plans
22 (0–8)	Social Security expenditure
23 (0–8)	Federal U.C. expenditure
24 (0–8)	State U.C. expenditure
25 (0–8)	Workmans compensation expenditures
26 (0–8)	Payments to other legally required plans

Table A4–1—*Continued*

Word Number	Description of Data
27–23	For B.L.S. use only
33–43	Not used
44 (0–8)	Vacation hours
45 (0–8)	Holiday hours
46 (0–8)	Sick leave hours
47 (0–8)	Civic and other leave hours
48–50	Not used
51 (0–4)	Not used
51 (5–8)	Scheduled weekly hours
52 (0–8)	Number of employees (same as word 3)

Number of employees receiving paid vacation

53 (0–8)	Employees receiving no vacation
53 (0-8)	Under 1 week
55 (0–8)	1–2 weeks
56 (0–8)	2–3 weeks
57 (0–8)	3–4 weeks
58	4–5 weeks
59	5 weeks and over
60	Not used
61	Number of paid holidays
(5–6)	Full days
(7–8)	Half days

Definition of codes in word 2

(1) *S.I.C. Code* as defined in the 1963 Edition of the Bureau of the Budgets Standard Industrial Classification Manual.
(2) *Employee Group Code* (*digit 4*)
Codes 1 and 3 do not apply
Code 2 represents nonsupervisory employees in nonmanufacturing establishments or production employees in manufacturing establishments.
(3) *Region Code* (*digit 5*) *as defined in B.L.S. SCP Publications*
1 = Northeast Region
2 = Southern Region
3 = Midwestern Region
4 = West Region
(4) *Establishment Size Code* (*digit 6*)
1 = Under 20 employees   5 = 250–499 employees
2 = 20–49 employees   6 = 500–999 employees
3 = 50–99 employees   7 = 1000–2499 employees
4 = 100–249 employees   8–9 = 2500 or more employees
(5) *Met–Nonmet Codes* (*digit 7*)
1 = Metropolitan area
2 = Nonmentropolitan area
(6) *Union–Nonunion Codes* (*digit 8*)
0 = Does not apply
1 = Majority of employees were unionized
2 = Majority of employees were not unionized

employees in nonmanufacturing industries were reported to us. All expenditure items refer to total establishment annual expenditures, while the employment figures refer to the average number of employees on the establishment payroll during 1966. In computing the variables used in our study, it is important to note that "words" 6–14 are included in gross payroll and "words" 15–26 are not.

Calculation of the Variables

1. $ABSEN = $ (word 46)/(word 5)

The ratio of paid sick leave hours to total man-hours paid for, was taken as a proxy for the absentee rate. This can be thought of as a "Say's law of absenteeism"; the supply of sick-leave hours creates its own demand. That is, within an industry we assume absenteeism is a constant multiple of paid sick leave.

2. $STD.HRS(1) = $ (word 51)/40

The question asked in the survey was "How many hours per week were normally worked by the majority of employees ... ?" $STD.HRS(1)$ often took on a value greater than one indicating that some employers were including regularly scheduled overtime in this figure. That is, due to the F.L.S.A. the true standard hours variable should never be greater than 40 hours per week in the manufacturing industries. Consequently, the following imperfect proxy was used in the reported empirical work:

$$STD.HRS1 = \begin{cases} 1 & \text{if } STD.HRS1 \geq 1 \\ 0 & \text{otherwise} \end{cases}$$

See Chapter 5 for an explanation of this variable.

3. $WAGE = \dfrac{\text{words } [4\text{–}6\text{–}7\text{–}8\text{–}9\text{–}11\text{–}12\text{–}13\text{–}14]}{\text{words } [5\text{–}44\text{–}45\text{–}46\text{–}47]}$

The payroll for hours actually worked (including only straight-time wage payments) divided by total man-hours actually worked yields a measure of the average straight-time hourly wage rate in the establishment. This variable relative to the industry mean wage was taken as a proxy for the quit rate. An alternative proxy considered was

$$INCOME = \text{(word 4)/(word 3)}$$

That is, the higher the annual income per man in an establishment relative to the industry mean, the lower the quit rate would be. Consequently, we would expect this variable to be negatively related to overtime. Actually, there is a strong positive correlation since those firms that pay high annual incomes do so partially because of the longer hours of their employees. The *WAGE* variable is therefore used as a proxy for the quit rate in the results reported here.

4. FIXED COSTS

$$FC1 = \frac{\text{words } [6 + 7 + 8 + 9 + 13 + 14] + \sum_{i=15}^{26} (\text{word } i)}{(\text{word } 3) \times 52}$$

Assuming that all "fringe benefit" costs are fixed costs and dividing the total annual firm payments by the number of employee-weeks yields a measure of the fixed costs per man per week.

$$FC2 = FC1 - \frac{\sum_{i=18}^{22} (\text{word } i)}{(\text{word } 3) \times 52}$$

Most payments into funds administered by unions are actually man-hour related. Similarly, social security payments are man-hour related of annual earnings per man were less than $6,600 in 1966. These items are consequently deducted from *FC1* to get an alternative measure of the fixed costs.

5. *RATIO*

Corresponding to these measures, three possible variables representing the ratio of weekly fixed costs per man to the overtime wage rate were constructed.

$$RATIO1 = FC1 \div [(\text{one and a half})(WAGE)]$$

RATIO1 assumes that all fringe benefit costs are fixed and that the overtime premium is uniformly time-and-a-half.

$$RATIO2 = FC2 \div \left[(\text{one and a half}) (WAGE) + \frac{\sum_{i=18}^{22} (\text{word } i)}{(\text{word } 5)} \right]$$

RATIO2 deducts those fringe benefits that may be man-hour related from the fixed costs and includes their hourly cost in the hourly overtime cost. Again, it is assumed that the overtime wage premium (which applies only to the wage rate—not the hourly fringes) is time-and-a-half.

$$
RATIO3 = FC2 \div \left[\frac{\text{word 11}}{\text{word 10}} (WAGE) + \frac{\sum\limits_{i=18}^{22} (\text{word } i)}{(\text{word 5})} \right] \quad \begin{array}{l} \text{if word } 10 > 0 \\ \text{if word } 10 = 0 \end{array}
$$

$$
= -1
$$

RATIO3 is essentially the same as *RATIO2* except that the overtime premium is calculated directly from the data. That is, if the overtime premium was time-and-a-half, we would expect that word 10 equal twice word 11.

If not, then we set the premium equal to word 11/(word 10). If the establishment has zero overtime payments at straight-time rates the variable is undefined. Consequently, we set its value equal to a negative number to indicate this, Obviously, all zero overtime establishments (less than 5 percent of the manufacturing establishments) must be eliminated from the sample when *RATIO3* is used.

6. *OVTIME*

Two definitions of annual observed overtime per man were calculated. Note that we are concerned only with overtime hours for which premium payments are received.

$$
OVTIME1 = \frac{(\text{word 11})}{(\text{one-half})(WAGE)(\text{word 3})}
$$

Annual overtime payments at premium rates divided by the overtime premium times the number of employees yields *OVTIME1*. This assumes that the overtime premium is one-half the wage rate.

$$
OVTIME2 = \frac{(\text{word 10})}{(\text{word 3})(WAGE)} \quad \text{if words 10 and 11} \neq 0
$$

$$
= 0 \quad \text{if words 10 or 11} = 0
$$

OVTIME2 essentially calculates the overtime premium from the data.

That is

$$OVTIME2 = \frac{(\text{word } 11)}{\dfrac{\text{word } 11}{\text{word } 10}} \, (WAGE)(\text{word } 3)$$

To be consistent with their definitions, three possible combinations of the various *OVTIME* and *RATIO* variables are permissible; (*OVTIME1*, *RATIO1*), (*OVTIME1*, *RATIO2*), (*OVTIME2*, *RATIO3*). While the latter combination is the theoretically most appropriate one, regressions using the various combinations yielded only marginally different results. Consequently, we report results only for the combination (*OVTIME1*, *RATIO1*) here. This combination was chosen since it is the only one of the three which allows us to calculate directly from the regression results, the effect of an increase in the overtime premium on overtime hours worked.

7. $NEWSEN = \dfrac{\text{words } [53 + 54]}{\text{words } [52-53-54]}$

As a proxy for the ratio of "new" to "senior" workers we take the ratio of those employees who receive less than one week paid vacation a year to those employees that receive at least one week of paid vacation a year.

8. $LABSEN = \dfrac{(\text{word } 5)}{\text{words } [52-53-54]}$

As a proxy for the ratio of "required labor services" to the number of senior workers, we take the ratio of total man-hours paid for to the number of employees that receive at least one week of paid vacation a year.

The following dummy variables were constructed from the information found in word 2 of the survey.

(a) $UNION = \begin{cases} 1 & \text{if the majority of the establishments employees were} \\ & \text{unionized} \\ 0 & \text{otherwise} \end{cases}$

(b) $ESCi = \begin{cases} 1 & \text{if the establishment is in size class } i \\ 0 & \text{otherwise} \quad (\text{for } i = 1, \ldots, 9) \end{cases}$

(c) $SICi$ $= \begin{cases} 1 & \text{if the establishment was in the three-digit industry} \\ & \text{that ended in } i \\ 0 & \text{otherwsie} \quad (\text{for } i = 2, \ldots, 9) \end{cases}$

All establishments were classified by three-digit industry code. The data was segmented into two-digit industry groups and the dummy variable approach used to indicate differences in overtime behavior across component three-digit manufacturing industries.

Also calculated but not utilized in the final regressions were dummy variables which indicated whether or not the establishment was in a metropolitan area, and in which of four broad geographic regions the establishment was located.

Appendix to Chapter 5

Homogenity of Variances and the Chow Test[1]

The Chow test, which we employ extensively throughout Chapters 5 and 6, is based upon the assumption that the true disturbance terms are normally distributed with mean zero and constant variance-covariance matrix $\sigma^2 I$ for each group. If the variances of the disturbance terms are not constant across groups, then the test is not strictly appropriate. The observations should first be standardized to assure the homogeneity of variances across groups, rather than estimating the within-group and overall regressions directly from the raw data. The problems caused by the nonhomogeneity of the group variances are similar, of course, to the problems caused by heteroscedastic residuals in a single within-group regression; ordinary least squares (OLS) estimates of the coefficients of the overall regression will remain unbiased, but they will no longer be minimum-variance among the class of linear estimators.

In this appendix, we test the homogeneity of the error variances assumption for our first application of the Chow test in Chapter 5. These regressions, reported in Table 5–1, were based on our basic model and estimated for each two-digit industry. Since the hypothesis of equal variance is rejected, we then discuss a more appropriate test of the hypothesis that the estimated set of regression coefficients is identical for all sixteen industries and indicate the results of conducting this test. Theoretically this procedure should be repeated for each application of the Chow test. However, given our arbitrary specification of the functional form to be estimated and our use of proxy variables, we do not believe that the effort at statistical sophistication would yield positive marginal returns after the first application. Consequently, it may be necessary to interpret the statements in the text concerning the rejection of the null hypothesis heuristically, rather than as formal statistical inferences.

An unbiased estimate of the variance of the disturbance term in a regression is the residual variance (s^2). For the regressions found in Table 5–1, the residual variances are listed in Table 5–8 for each industry. Also listed are the number of degrees of freedom in each within-industry regression, the number of observations minus the number of regression coefficients minus one (n_i).

Inspection of Table A5.8 leads one to believe that the assumption of

---

[1] I am indebted to Professor E. Savin for suggesting that the work presented in this appendix be undertaken. He is in no way responsible for the views expressed here however.

homogeneity of error variances across the manufacturing industries may be inappropriate. Under the assumption of normality of the disturbances, one possible test statistic is,[2]

$$\lambda = -2 \log_e u \bigg/ \left[1 + \frac{1}{3(k-1)} \left(\sum_{i=1}^{k} \frac{1}{n_i - 1} - \frac{1}{n-k} \right) \right] \qquad (A5.1)$$

where k is the number of subgroups (here 16) and

$$u = \prod_{i=1}^{k} \left(\frac{n_i s_i^2}{n_i - 1} \right)^{n_i - 1/2} \left[\frac{\sum_{i=1}^{k} n_i s_i^2}{\sum_{i=1}^{k} (n_i - 1)} \right]^{\sum_{i=1}^{k} n_i - 1/2} \qquad (A5.2)$$

λ is distributed approximately as a Chi-square variable with $k-1$ degrees of freedom and high values of λ imply a rejection of the null hypothesis that the variance of the true residuals is constant across groups.[3] Computation of the desired statistic indicates that $\hat{\lambda} = 138.481$ with 15 degrees of freedom. This is greater than the critical value of 32.8 at the 0.995 level of significance and consequently we reject the null hypothesis.

Given this nonhomogeneity of the error variance across industries, the data must be transformed before the Chow test is performed. To standardize the variance of the disturbance term in the overall regression, for each observation in the ith industry all the variables should be divided by $\sqrt{s_i^2}$.[4] That is, ordinary least squares applied to this transformed data yields the appropriate generalized least squares estimate for the original data. The estimated weighted overall regression is found in Table A5-9. Not only do the coefficients differ in magnitude from the unweighted overall regression found in Table 5-1, but the coefficient of the *STD.HRS* variable is actually now negative and significant. The residual sum of squares obtained from this regression is the theoretically correct measure of Q_1 for our Chow test (see page 66).

The transformed data should also be used in each of the within-industry regressions. However, going back to the intraindustry results presented in Table 5-1, dividing each observation's set of variables in industry i by the same number $(\sqrt{s_i^2})$ will not alter the estimated regression coefficients. However, the residual sum of squares would be modified, and in fact, the

---

[2] This test is unfortunately not robust with respect to departures from normality. On this see Scheffe [62], p. 337.

[3] This test is presented in Hoel [34], p. 225–228.

[4] This procedure assumes homoscedastic residuals within an industry.

residual sum of squares for the regressions with the transformed data are exactly equal to the residual sum of squares for the regressions with the original data divided by the estimated residual variance (s_i^2) for that regression. Consequently, it is not necessary to reestimate any of the within-industry regressions in order to obtain the theoretically appropriate measure of the within-industry residual sum of squares.

Given the "corrected" residual sum of squares for both the overall and within-group regressions a Chow test was then performed. Computations indicate an F statistic of 39.961 with (105, 891) degrees of freedom. This is again sufficiently large to reject the hypothesis that the set of regression coefficients are identical for all the manufacturing industries.

Table A5-1. Intercept Varies with Establishment Size: OLS Estimates (t ratios in parentheses)

$$OT = \sum_{i=1}^{9} \alpha_i ESC. + \beta_1 RATIO + \beta_2 STD.HRS + \beta_3 WAGE + \beta_4 ABSEN + \beta_5 NEWSEN + \beta_6 UNION$$

Industry Number	Number of Observations	RATIO	STD.HRS	WAGE	NEWSEN	ABSEN	UNION	R^2	F
20	77	23.307[a] (1.938)	-11.553 (-0.069)	-47.105 (-1.516)	0.114 (1.184)	-2386.400 (-0.748)	-0.557 (-0.012)	0.238	8.866
22	137	36.294[c] (4.096)	130.210 (1.591)	-51.112 (-0.926)	0.009 (1.042)	-7651.600[b] (-2.029)	-49.144[b] (-2.162)	0.237	31.759
23	126	5.063[c] (3.673)	-29.372[b] (-1.997)	2.298 (0.209)	-0.036[a] (-1.895)	-768.140 (-0.209)	-31.077 (-2.112)	0.220	14.667
24	25	20.673 (0.940)		-43.592 (-0.830)	0.067 (0.941)	-9274.100 (1.280)	-63.047 (-0.822)	0.630	8.099
25	23	39.848 (1.251)	-172.88 (-1.123)	-127.550[a] (-1.960)	-0.156 (-0.803)	-9960.400 (-1.413)	82.616 (0.744)	0.603	3.059
26	33	80.663[b] (2.043)	68.408 (0.287)	-96.640 (-0.993)	141.790 (1.164)	4188.600 (0.329)	112.120 (1.127)	0.438	7.031
27	35	27.577 (1.537)	-41.516 (-0.691)	-20.408 (-0.737)	137.490[b] (2.205)	2096.900 (0.537)	12.526 (0.169)	0.409	4.281
28	38	24.573 (1.563)		-23.686 (-0.637)	0.294 (1.823)	3642.900 (1.214)	145.010[b] (2.498)	0.423	7.957
30	24	50.747[b] (2.694)		58.678 (0.703)	0.227 (1.532)	-121.580 (-0.024)	-44.298 (-0.633)	0.620	8.231

Table A5-1—Continued

	N							R^2	F
32	108	9.297 (0.789)	-17.542 (-0.121)	-71.998[b] (-1.995)	-0.222[b] (-2.016)	9079.400 (0.663)	59.291 (0.958)	0.140	15.523
33	77	25.934[b] (2.699)		-63.763 (-1.387)	0.259[a] (1.768)	-624.090 (-1.383)	0.442 (0.009)	0.235	23.172
34	92	25.964[b] (2.287)		-53.482 (-1.445)	0.042 (0.361)	-2607.300[a] (-0.979)	9.046 (0.220)	0.191	15.995
35	79	33.696[c] (3.657)	124.960 (1.095)	-28.888 (-0.928)	-4.371 (-1.394)	-2156.400 (-0.645)	13.254 (0.301)	0.387	20.605
36	61	33.967[c] (3.771)	29.517 (0.399)	3.284 (0.171)	11.611 (1.201)	-2311.700 (-1.287)	-62.020[b] (-2.179)	0.317	12.782
37	47	-1.972 (-0.164)	289.620[b] (2.438)	-13.930 (-0.296)	10.667[c] (3.583)	-4322.200 (-1.256)	-0.611 (-0.017)	0.446	14.178
39	21	70.611[a] (1.792)	-268.100 (-1.294)	-70.761 (-1.128)	5.288 (0.371)	-4573.000 (-0.415)	-70.624	0.662	3.725
All Manufacturing	1,003	14.994[c] (6.885)	57.227[c] (2.964)	-0.735 (-0.095)	-0.048 (-0.193)	-1850.700[b] (-2.091)	-34.442[c] (-3.208)	0.080	6.138

[a] Coefficient statistically significantly different from zero at the 0.90 level of significance; two-tailed test.
[b] Coefficient statistically significantly different from zero at the 0.95 level of significance; two-tailed test.
[c] Coefficient statistically significantly different from zero at the 0.99 level of significance; two-tailed test.

Table A5–2. Two-Stage Least Square Estimates: NEWSEN Equation   (t ratios in parentheses)

$$NEWSEN = b_0 + b_1 RATIO + b_2 STD.HRS + b_3 WAGE + b_4 LABSEN + b_5 ABSEN + b_6 UNION$$

Industry Number	Number of Observations	RATIO	STD.HRS	WAGE	LABSEN	ABSEN	UNION	Constant	R^2
20	77	-2.088[b] (-1.982)	4.038 (0.268)	2.168 (0.773)	0.00043[c] (114.59)	-7.697 (-0.027)	0.964 (0.243)	0.630 (0.042)	0.994
22	137	-0.075 (-1.003)	-0.239 (-0.055)	0.230 (0.487)	0.00045[c] (1374.300)	6.881 (0.231)	-0.0079 (-0.041)	-1.024 (-0.898)	0.999
23	126	-0.093 (-0.755)	1.269 (1.035)	0.323 (0.362)	0.00049[c] (622.870)	59.432 (0.188)	0.156 (0.127)	-2.334 (-1.037)	0.999
24	25	1.586 (0.312)		3.791 (0.336)	0.00044[c] (59.549)	-103.270 (-0.062)	17.744 (1.011)	-22.279 (-0.785)	0.995
25	23	0.022 (0.846)	0.042 (0.309)	0.038 (0.790)	0.00049[c] (6379.5)	1.318 (0.223)	0.053 (0.718)	-1.353[c] (-6.563)	1.000
26	33	-0.049[c] (-3.622)	-0.068 (-0.725)	-0.007 (-0.253)	0.00041[c] (20.719)	1.942 (0.350)	-0.051 (-1.257)	-0.551[c] (-2.995)	0.969
27	35	-0.019[a] (-1.919)	0.018 (0.535)	0.007 (0.417)	0.00040[c] (26.102)	-0.805 (-0.381)	-0.031 (-0.820)	-0.760[c] (-8.431)	0.972
28	38	-0.014[b] (-1.991)		0.009 (0.004)	0.00044[c] (11339.0)	-0.158 (-0.097)	-0.064[b] (-2.015)	-0.826[c] (10.712)	1.000
30	24	-0.021 (-1.380)		-0.031 (-0.062)	0.00045[c] (7333.0)	-1.404[c] (-2.954)	-0.0075 (-0.118)	-0.787[c] (-7.228)	1.000
32	108	-0.906 (-0.916)	-0.8781 (-0.061)	-0.818 (-0.233)	0.00046[c] (102.940)	156.22 (0.117)	-0.981 (-0.169)	8.651 (0.508)	0.993
33	77	-0.013[b] (-2.178)		-0.002 (-0.096)	0.00043[c] (10810.0)	-1.278 (-0.4421)	-0.003 (-0.114)	-0.842[c] (12.808)	1.000
34	92	-0.337 (-0.355)		-4.890[a] (-1.671)	0.00045[c] (98.828)	32.008 (0.138)	2.017 (0.579)	12.534 (1.569)	0.992
35	79	-0.024 (-1.408)	-0.111 (-0.501)	-0.007 (-0.109)	0.00047[c] (166.310)	4.609 (0.701)	0.038 (0.503)	-0.886[c] (-2.974)	0.997
36	61	-0.022[c] (-3.896)	0.017 (0.407)	0.003 (0.279)	0.00047[c] (192.03)	1.325 (1.189)	0.024 (1.499)	-0.924[c] (-15.090)	0.995
37	47	-0.009 (-0.043)		1.007 (1.374)	0.00049[c] (408.74)	-1.616 (0.027)	0.664 (0.718)	-4.720[c] (-2.276)	0.999
39	21	0.0005 (0.053)		0.001 (0.001)	0.00045[c] (42.127)	-1.194 (-0.518)	-0.047 (-0.932)	-0.965[c] (-5.536)	0.996

[a] Coefficient statistically significantly different from zero at the 0.90 level of significance; two-tailed test.
[b] Coefficient statistically significantly different from zero at the 0.95 level of significance; two-tailed test.
[c] Coefficient statistically significantly different from zero at the 0.99 level of significance; two-tailed test.

Table A5-3. Basic Model: Two-Stage Least Square Estimates   (t ratios in parentheses)

$$OT = \beta_0 + \beta_1 RATIO + \beta_2 STD.HRS + \beta_3 WAGE + \beta_4 NEWSEN + \beta_5 ABSEN + \beta_6 UNION$$

Industry Number	Number of Observations	STD.HRS	RATIO	WAGE	NEWSEN	ABSEN	UNION	Constant
20	77	26.385[b] (2.298)	15.409 (0.093)	-51.471[a] (-1.684)	0.088 (0.934)	-3108.100 (-1.035)	-32.078 (-0.743)	179.530 (1.089)
22	137	29.908[c] (3.318)	128.920 (1.512)	-57.347 (-1.011)	0.047 (0.538)	-6568.200[a] (-1.834)	-39.367[a] (-1.698)	69.109 (0.504)
23	126	5.145[c] (3.810)	-27.975[b] (-2.098)	7.777 (0.799)	-0.040[b] (-2.309)	-2022.600 (-0.587)	-35.272[b] (-2.641)	79.743[c] (3.244)
24	25	10.896 (0.486)		-38.449 (-0.772)	0.049 (0.670)	-7035.200 (-0.960)	-103.000 (-1.337)	278.740[b] (2.233)
25	23	21.961 (0.834)	-58.716 (-0.424)	-57.339 (-1.142)	-0.100 (-0.626)	-7395.200 (-1.231)	-40.259 (-0.536)	264.820 (1.259)
26	33	108.920[c] (3.336)	149.430 (0.728)	-18.192 (-0.282)	201.350[a] (1.933)	4090.100 (-0.341)	120.110 (1.333)	-546.270 (-1.508)
27	35	32.769[b] (2.086)	-19.058 (-0.374)	-16.747 (-0.653)	199.180[c] (3.459)	1885.000 (0.594)	35.940 (0.620)	-14.915 (-0.142)
28	38	25.810[b] (2.079)		-9.698 (-0.263)	0.216 (1.465)	990.270 (0.366)	126.560[b] (2.375)	-43.233 (-0.335)
30	24	40.430[c] (2.953)		20.406 (0.449)	0.113 (0.935)	2602.700 (0.616)	-17.538 (-0.313)	-48.293 (-0.499)
32	108	11.766 (1.215)	-54.938 (.394)	-61.217[a] (-1.791)	-0.085 (0.891)	2876.700 (0.221)	59.447 (1.082)	452.100[c] (2.718)
33	77	16.570[a] (1.841)		-65.373[a] (-1.729)	0.229 (1.690)	1876.500 (0.441)	-34.959 (-0.795)	331.140[c] (3.428)
34	92	26.938[b] (2.539)		-53.972[a] (-1.655)	0.088 (0.781)	-3088.200 (-1.197)	-7.185 (-0.185)	210.010[b] (2.359)
35	79	33.752[c] (3.789)	126.430 (1.092)	-39.659 (-1.238)	-0.189 (-0.606)	-2878.500 (-0.842)	-16.969 (-0.426)	81.674 (0.527)
36	61	33.283[c] (3.721)	-37.010 (-0.543)	5.154 (0.254)	6.517 (0.787)	-1726.400 (-0.974)	-49.864[a] (-1.930)	25.435 (0.267)
37	47	4.977 (0.339)		-40.715 (-0.816)	-0.201 (-1.208)	-4874.700 (-1.182)	15.338 (0.243)	321.970[b] (2.282)
39	21	53.153[a] (2.062)	-68.805 (-0.406)	-18.622 (-0.365)	4.296 (0.423)	-1510.000 (-0.406)	-35.278 (-0.385)	215.900 (0.096)

[a] Coefficient statistically significantly different from zero at the 0.90 level of significance; two-tailed test.
[b] Coefficient statistically significantly different from zero at the 0.95 level of significance; two-tailed test.
[c] Coefficient statistically significantly different from zero at the 0.99 level of significance; two-tailed test.

Table A5–4. Intercept Varies with Establishment Size: Two-Stage Least Square Estimates (t ratios in parentheses)

$$OT = \sum_{i=1}^{9} \alpha_i ESC_i + \beta_1 RATIO + \beta_2 STD.HRS + \beta_3 WAGE + \beta_4 NE\hat{W}SEN + \beta_5 ABSEN + \beta_6 UNION$$

Industry Number	Number of Observations	RATIO	STD.HRS	WAGE	NEŴSEN	ABSEN	UNION
20	77	23.229[a] (1.931)	-12.396 (-0.074)	-46.999 (-1.521)	0.123 (1.280)	-2358.300 (-0.739)	-0.021 (-0.004)
22	137	36.314[c] (4.098)	130.021 (1.591)	-51.003 (-0.920)	0.093 (1.055)	-7655.500[b] (-2.211)	-49.148[b] (-2.162)
23	126	5.073[c] (3.643)	-29.241[b] (-1.987)	2.336 (0.212)	-0.035[a] (-1.862)	-752.600 (-0.204)	-31.108[b] (-2.114)
24	25	21.118 (0.960)		-44.480 (-0.847)	0.071 (0.996)	-927.200 (-1.280)	-61.513 (-0.802)
25	23	39.881 (1.252)	-172.860 (-1.123)	-127.530[a] (-1.960)	-0.156 (-0.801)	-9960.800 (-1.413)	82.628 (0.744)
26	33	99.652[c] (2.429)	83.643 (0.340)	-89.773 (-0.893)	278.400[b] (2.142)	4439.800 (0.338)	145.210 (1.410)
27	35	34.196[a] (1.869)	-35.911 (-0.588)	-15.568 (-0.553)	188.520[c] (2.922)	2148.900 (0.541)	6.630 (0.088)

Table A5–4—*Continued*

28	38	24.575 (1.563)		−23.689 (−0.637)	0.294 (1.825)	3643.900 (1.214)	145.060[b] (2.498)
30	24	50.745[b] (2.695)		58.696 (0.703)	0.227 (1.534)	−122.670 (−0.024)	44.300 (−0.633)
32	108	14.009 (1.368)	−26.718 (−0.191)	−51.094 (−1.471)	−0.218[b] (−2.067)	5769.900 (0.441)	89.873 (1.515)
33	77	23.432[b] (2.499)		−65.699 (−1.414)	0.257 (1.734)	+483.100 (−0.106)	3.497 (0.069)
34	92	26.402[b] (2.324)		−53.540 (−1.446)	0.061 (0.515)	−2757.500 (−0.967)	9.709 (0.237)
35	79	33.641[c] (3.650)	12.480 (1.094)	−28.569 (−0.918)	−3.917 (−1.248)	−2173.00 (−0.649)	12.137 (0.276)
36	62	31.745[c] (3.326)	−2.449 (−0.030)	−6.278 (−0.285)	12.555 (1.272)	−2079.800 (−1.141)	−65.430[b] (−2.272)
37	47	−2.829 (−0.203)		−27.169 (−0.489)	10.817[c] (3.068)	−4522.500 (−1.109)	23.096 (0.366)
39	21	71.115[a] (1.804)	−270.320 (−1.304)	−71.556 (−1.141)	6.274 (0.440)	−4545.200 (−1.436)	−64.692 (−0.380)

[a] Coefficient statistically significantly different from zero at 0.90 level of significance; two-tailed test.
[b] Coefficient statistically significantly different from zero at 0.95 level of significance; two-tailed test.
[c] Coefficient statistically significantly different from zero at 0.99 level of significance; two-tailed test.

Table A5–5. Intercept Terms for Regressions in Table A5–4

Size Class	20	22	23	Industry 24	25	26	27	28
ESC1	417.17[b]		118.65[c]	251.75	340.27[a]	−394.59	7.61	−3.323
ESC2	196.22	−108.65	77.88[b]	179.15	457.96[a]	−524.51	−84.51	−80.724
ESC3	179.95	−23.46	84.26[c]	270.75[a]	279.38	−343.07	27.49	−58.719
ESC4	199.59	47.09	79.26[c]	386.16[c]	314.09	−325.15	67.95	111.820
ESC5	128.56	21.41	87.91[c]	152.99	330.49	−264.50	−6.52	−95.244
ESC6	149.02	53.24	93.82[c]	86.22	250.70	−305.71	−78.07	2.032
ESC7	220.09	67.57	95.03[c]	259.93	442.74	−212.00	68.34	−70.459
ESC8	206.09	190.48	116.02[a]		490.09[a]	60.64	−6.19	−89.120
ESC9		−418.58					−0.06	

[a] Coefficient statistically significantly different from zero at 0.90 level of significance; two-tailed test.
[b] Coefficient statistically significantly different from zero at 0.95 level of significance; two-tailed test.
[c] Coefficient statistically significantly different from zero at 0.99 level of significance; two-tailed test.

			Industry				
30	32	33	34	35	36	37	39
	630.79[c]		170.53	−46.74	58.22	−1073.4[c]	218.64
−84.39	500.95	144.10	292.90[b]	116.10	−29.90	196.03	266.55
−166.43	328.15	402.77[a]	236.01[b]	30.110	−51.22		156.19
−157.56	405.65	315.30[b]	138.32	167.69	3.15	317.48[b]	431.41
−251.84	366.09	274.74[b]	189.40	28.904	12.39	256.09	269.97
−228.57	373.05	310.59[b]	237.99[a]	−4.06	33.73	231.14	516.86
−156.56	367.86	228.10[b]	162.64	15.43	67.37	379.79[a]	222.03
−198.54	381.45	243.90[a]	245.48	−50.36	84.00	379.32[b]	71.11
		209.71		−52.86	94.31	289.37	

Table A5-6. Intercept and Ratio Coefficient Vary with ESC (*t* ratios in parentheses)

$$OT = \sum_{j=1}^{9} \gamma_j D_j + \sum_{j=1}^{9} \alpha_j D_j RATIO + b_1 STD.HRS + b_2 WAGE + b_3 NEWSEN + b_4 ABSEN + b_5 UNION$$

Industry Number	Number of Observations	STD.HRS	WAGE	NEWSEN	ABSEN	UNION	R^2	F
20	77	-6.098 (-0.037)	-42.023 (-1.438)	0.131 (1.471)	-4825.400 (-1.455)	19.172 (0.443)	0.440	8.148
22	137	132.100[a] (1.692)	-60.122 (-1.113)	0.291 (0.318)	-8950.400[b] (-2.105)	-54.642[b] (-2.461)	0.335	26.852
23	126	-27.459[a] (-1.871)	4.599 (0.396)	-0.004[b] (-2.075)	-1227.600 (-0.330)	-29.351[a] (-1.826)	0.285	11.085
24	25		-64.183 (-1.065)	0.013 (0.163)	1049.200 (0.480)	87.816 (0.712)	0.807	5.948
25	23	-184.090 (-0.909)	-122.700 (-1.098)	-0.067 (-0.101)	-233.850 (-0.006)	96.106 (0.421)	0.638	1.477
26	33	64.597 (0.206)	-130.004 (-1.151)	-9.438 (-0.054)	6349.00 (0.459)	163.340 (1.091)	0.581	4.736
27	35	-168.820[b] (-2.661)	-62.053[b] (-2.457)	-98.437 (-1.109)	-1428.600[b] (-2.515)	-42.626 (-0.646)	0.779	5.335

Table A5–6—Continued

28	38		8.511 (0.215)	0.332[b] (2.227)	5880.000[a] (1.814)	178.810[b] (2.952)	0.637	7.186
30	24		42.277 (0.396)	0.113 (0.777)	−1834.300 (−0.250)	−27.416 (−0.340)	0.842	7.068
32	108	−191.740 (−0.135)	−72.572[b] (−2.041)	−0.189[a] (−1.891)	1585.700 (1.140)	31.264 (0.490)	0.242	12.124
33	77		−64.106 (−1.387)	0.271[a] (1.889)	−1184.400[b] (−2.194)	−7.967 (−0.161)	0.416	18.466
34	92		−50.841 (−1.308)	0.144 (0.986)	−2561.700 (−0.915)	8.951 (0.205)	0.223	10.686
35	79	112.920 (0.940)	−18.418 (−0.566)	−3.922 (−1.224)	−2160.200 (−0.662)	15.965 (0.337)	0.459	13.627
36	61	−115.520 (−1.023)	−6.111 (−0.257)	4.084 (0.189)	−2578.700 (−1.288)	−61.207[a] (−1.913)	0.384	7.679
37	47	255.050 (1.461)	−20.181 (−0.412)	9.968[b] (2.719)	−6056.000 (−1.627)	7.031 (0.115)	0.576	10.874
39	21	−103.030 (−1.470)	7.385 (0.270)	11.111 (0.295)	8160.700[b] (3.745)	212.100 (0.379)	0.989	37.925

[a] Coefficient statistically significantly different from zero at 0.90 level of significance; two-tailed test.
[b] Coefficient statistically significantly different from zero at 0.95 level of significance; two-tailed test.
[c] Coefficient statistically significantly different from zero at 0.99 level of significance; two-tailed test.
Ratio and intercept coefficients for this regression are listed in Table 5–6.

Table A–57. Union–Nonunion Comparisons (t statistics in parentheses)

$$OT = b_0 + b_1 RATIO + b_2 STD.HRS + b_3 WAGE + b_4 NEWSEN + b_5 ABSEN$$

Industry Number	Number of Observations	RATIO	STD.HRS	WAGE	NEWSEN	ABSEN	Constant	R^2	F
20(A)	77	25.251[b] (2.241)	4.890 (0.003)	−59.742[b] (−2.097)	0.086 (0.921)	−3079.000 (−1.029)	193.660 (1.186)	0.128	2.077
20(N)	28	51.138[b] (2.002)	56.433 (0.253)	−190.530[b] (−2.282)	−0.052 (−0.315)	−1846.800 (−1.382)	329.390 (1.384)	0.268	1.614
20(U)	49	20.371[a] (1.913)		−15.633 (−0.603)	0.103 (0.876)	−3025.400 (−1.303)	101.380 (1.383)	0.121	1.502
22(A)	137	25.882[c] (2.954)	134.220 (1.564)	−47.331 (−1.321)	0.048 (0.549)	−5483.500 (−1.545)	97.312 (0.710)	0.092	2.657
22(N)	92	22.901[b] (2.071)	141.750 (1.282)	−160.960[b] (−2.444)	0.008 (0.093)	−4388.900 (−1.268)	267.500 (1.614)	0.129	2.546
22(U)	45	38.096[b] (2.382)	137.120 (0.987)	120.630 (1.125)	−5.307 (−0.055)	−7472.800 (−0.826)	−344.380 (1.344)	0.186	1.782
23(A)	126	4.384[c] (3.242)	−24.112[a] (−1.777)	−3.334 (−0.371)	−0.044[b] (−2.435)	373.260 (0.109)	78.604[b] (3.122)	0.158	4.491
23(N)	39	9.395 (0.845)	−14.768 (−0.405)	−19.174 (−0.750)	−0.005 (−1.470)	−3895.500 (−0.790)	100.340 (1.301)	0.131	0.996
23(U)	87	4.979[c] (3.711)	−31.095[b] (−2.045)	13.837 (1.240)	−0.039 (−1.879)	−1808.500 (−0.326)	33.716 (1.121)	0.255	5.356
32(A)	108	10.907 (0.991)	−38.860 (0.268)	−76.327[b] (−2.304)	−0.095 (−1.076)	6369.000 (0.475)	384.900[b] (2.253)	0.052	1.124
32(N)	11	12.009 (0.190)		14.350 (0.078)	−0.067 (−0.391)	−6045.400 (−0.429)	163.030 (0.509)	0.072	0.117
32(U)	97	18.132[a] (1.632)	−52.420 (−0.387)	−76.892[b] (−2.135)	92.856[b] (2.582)	7445.300 (0.583)	351.300 (2.065)	0.125	2.617

Table A5-7—Continued

33(A)	77	20.486[b] (2.211)		−73.306[b] (−2.082)	0.234[a] (1.781)	1801.100 (0.429)	326.270[c] (3.454)	0.102	2.039
33(N)	10	8.606 (0.487)		−97.232 (−0.753)	−43.538 (−1.428)	−526.870 (−0.023)	516.510 (1.524)	0.340	0.646
33(U)	67	35.469[b] (2.584)		−82.274[b] (−2.026)	0.304[b] (2.155)	2335.800 (0.538)	268.610[b] (2.363)	0.127	2.263
34(A)	92	25.806[b] (2.531)		−55.705[a] (−1.825)	0.069 (0.627)	−3025.500 (−1.205)	216.410[b] (2.478)	0.101	2.435
34(N)	29	41.402[a] (1.782)		−67.720 (−1.040)	0.103 (0.725)	−4056.200 (−0.928)	176.730 (0.914)	0.168	1.210
34(U)	63	17.067 (1.325)		−38.521 (−0.997)	2.873 (0.532)	−3473.200 (−0.955)	220.620 (1.884)	0.074	1.169
35(A)	79	33.672[c] (3.804)	131.370 (1.146)	−44.632 (−1.448)	−2.733 (−0.899)	−2435.800 (−0.759)	82.001 (0.532)	0.220	4.130
35(N)	36	39.517[c] (3.467)		−88.821[a] (−1.998)	−3.981 (−0.233)	−2180.400 (−0.545)	301.200[b] (2.399)	0.352	4.213
35(U)	43	12.099 (0.737)	219.890[b] (2.007)	51.445 (1.092)	−2.108 (−0.726)	3349.100 (0.349)	−170.230 (−0.875)	0.163	1.449
36(A)	61	28.863[c] (3.218)	−43.133 (−0.619)	1.012 (0.049)	6.195 (0.736)	−926.090 (−0.522)	33.188 (0.341)	0.181	2.434
36(N)	25	49.745[c] (2.803)	−105.940 (−0.911)	3.021 (0.076)	8.652 (0.832)	−3404.500 (−1.088)	20.847 (0.114)	0.381	2.342
36(U)	36	23.124[b] (2.291)	29.900 (0.335)	10.317 (0.442)	61.476 (1.223)	−1111.500 (−0.515)	−60.649 (−0.522)	0.188	1.389

[a] Coefficient statistically significantly different from zero at 0.90 level of significance; two-tailed test.
[b] Coefficient statistically significantly different from zero at 0.95 level of significance; two-tailed test.
(A) All establishments, (N) nonunionized only, (U) unionized only.

Table A5–8. Residual Variances from Table 5-1

S.I.C. Code	s_i^2	n_i	S.I.C. Code	s_i^2	n_i
20	2.527	69	30	1.291	16
22	1.424	129	32	2.075	100
23	0.340	118	33	1.404	69
24	1.974	17	34	2.195	84
25	1.708	15	35	2.443	71
26	3.651	25	36	0.862	53
27	1.482	27	37	1.422	39
28	1.833	30	39	1.866	13

Note: All residual variances should be multiplied by 10^4.

Table A5–9. Basic Model: Overall Weighted Regression

	RATIO	STD.HRS	WAGE	NEWSEN	ABSEN	UNION	Constant	R^2	F
Coefficient	8.282	−20.254	−6.641	−0.033	−1454.734	−29.052	162.489	0.058	10.226
t statistic	(6.64)[c]	(−2.074)[b]	(−1.267)	(−2.300)[b]	(−1.785)[a]	(−3.441)[c]			

[a] Coefficient statistically significantly different from zero at the 0.90 level of significance; two-tailed test.
[b] Coefficient statistically significantly different from zero at the 0.95 level of significance; two-tailed test.
[c] Coefficient statistically significantly different from zero at the 0.99 level of significance; two-tailed test.

Appendix to Chapter 6

Table A6-1. Intercept Varies with Establishment Size—OLS Estimates (*t* ratios in parentheses)

$$OT = \sum_{i=1}^{9} \alpha_i ESC_i + \beta_1 RATIO + \beta_2 STD.HRS + \beta_3 WAGE + \beta_4 NEWSEN + \beta_5 ABSEN + \beta_6 UNION$$

Industry	Number of Observations	RATIO	STD.HRS	WAGE	NEWSEN	ABSEN	UNION	R^2	F
Mining	37	-0.531 (-0.055)	41.545 (0.288)	-51.285 (1.223)	0.107 (1.514)	-4573.200[a] (-1.828)	-66.668 (-1.193)	0.542	2.096
Construction	285	31.483[c] (6.032)	3.761 (0.102)	-29.065[b] (-2.521)	0.011 (0.537)	-2781.000 (-0.486)	-25.314 (-0.982)	0.153	3.783
Transportation	239	47.607[c] (5.988)	177.520 (1.097)	-32.153 (-1.597)	0.086[a] (1.650)	689.160 (0.224)	3.002 (0.082)	0.220	4.520
Utilities	184	10.197[b] (2.538)	-56.676[a] (-1.686)	-6.964 (-0.536)	-13.986 (-0.483)	136.790 (0.166)	16.807 (1.324)	0.129	1.783
Wholesale trade	244	39.403[c] (6.289)	56.113 (0.926)	-99.466[c] (-5.235)	-0.025 (-0.344)	-2990.800[b] (-2.048)	1.954 (0.062)	0.251	5.472
Retail trade	172	33.651[b] (4.402)	59.538[a] (1.718)	-16.821 (-0.950)	0.146[b] (2.415)	1322.700 (0.787)	-23.380 (-0.893)	0.217	3.109
Services	89	36.830[c] (3.861)	-25.496 (-0.687)	15.657 (1.018)	-0.028 (-0.574)	-1483.900 (-0.835)	-23.769 (-0.874)	0.299	2.470
Financial	25	20.740 (1.371)	-49.433 (-0.838)	-37.028 (-0.511)	-1.928 (-0.122)	-440.710 (-0.158)	157.930 (1.442)	0.590	1.221

[a] Coefficient statistically significantly different from zero at the 0.90 level of significance; two-tailed test.
[b] Coefficient statistically significantly different from zero at the 0.95 level of significance; two-tailed test.
[c] Coefficient statistically significantly different from zero at the 0.99 level of significance; two-tailed test.

Table A6–2. Basic Model—Data Segmented by Establishment Size (t ratios in parentheses)

$$OT = a_0 + a_1\,RATIO + a_2\,STDHRS + a_3\,WAGE + a_4\,NEWSEN + a_5\,ABSEN + a_6\,UNION$$

Industry	Number of Observations	RATIO	STD.HRS	WAGE	NEWSEN	ABSEN	UNION	Constant	R^2	F
Construction										
ESC1	63	15.401 (1.372)	100.880 (0.955)	-34.185 (-1.459)	-0.021 (-0.357)	-2748.400 (-0.880)	-43.967 (0.894)	107.980	0.163	1.818
ESC2	58	29.086[b] (2.527)	28.317 (0.450)	-21.650 (-0.858)	0.034 (0.766)	1063.300 (0.099)	-1.453 (-0.024)	29.009 (0.254)	0.138	1.368
ESC3	55	5.601 (0.475)	-88.024 (-1.289)	-31.557 (-1.398)	0.003 (0.071)	-5850.010 (-0.389)	-34.789 (-0.691)	30.964[b] (2.483)	0.095	0.847
ESC4	50	46.803[c] (3.108)	94.835 (0.540)	-25.771 (-0.607)	0.015 (0.209)	-1115.400 (-0.385)	40.922 (0.416)	-38.970 (-1.692)	0.204	1.839
ESC5	25	48.068[c] (3.001)	36.507 (0.364)	-46.258 (-1.385)	0.005 (0.752)		-27.755 (-0.031)	101.900 (0.621)	0.408	2.069
ESC6	21	19.161 (1.084)	-91.612 (-1.097)	16.230 (0.342)	0.126[a] (1.886)	1155.80 (1.260)	-184.740 (-2.460)	136.890 (0.654)	0.507	2.401
ESC7-8	13	73.887[c] (4.415)		-57.498 (-1.726)	-0.157[c] (3.000)	-2014.60 (-0.836)	-94.956 (-1.357)	299.340[a] (1.943)	0.827	6.703
Transportation										
ESC1	43	65.605[c] (3.795)		-92.857[a] (-1.889)	0.097 (1.147)	-6089.900 (-0.886)	-40.101 (-0.486)	165.440 (1.124)	0.341	3.828
ESC2	38	47.227[a] (1.846)		-49.341 (-0.924)	0.085 (0.611)	3436.800 (0.306)	32.645 (0.357)	63.557 (0.357)	0.203	1.637
ESC3	35	30.242[a] (1.768)	35.362	0.048 (0.706)	-2667.400 (0.261)	50.074 (0.604)	-116.150 (0.715)	0.275 (0.275)	0.275	2.211
ESC4	30	38.165 (1.239)		-113.160 (-1.280)	-1.273 (-0.046)	1638.000 (0.263)	62.742 (0.435)	244.800 (1.053)	0.134	0.746
ESC5	17	-47.345 (-0.807)		-101.270 (-1.179)	-29.640 (-1.671)	1208.400 (0.941)	421.370 (1.654)	417.600 (0.836)	0.367	1.275
ESC6	17	95.886[b] (2.226)		39.289 (0.393)	-224.730 (-1.383)	2126.900 (0.934)	-74.377 (-0.233)	-520.150 (-1.272)	0.637	3.869

		(1)	(2)	(3)	(4)	(5)	(6)	(7)	R^2	
ESC7	22	21.208 (0.550)		−17.876 (−0.287)	−255.390 (1.054)	1041.200 (0.919)	−132.100 (−0.844)	206.630 (0.481)	0.267	1.170
ESC8	14	80.038 (0.997)	156.080 (1.087)	200.450 (1.250)	140.860 (0.941)	3307.400 (1.443)		−1212.100 (−1.132)	0.378	0.975
ESC9	23	−7.929 (−0.477)		72.501 (1.011)	−76.825 (−0.952)	3.268 (0.006)		−49.168 (0.163)	0.133	0.692

Utilities

		(1)	(2)	(3)	(4)	(5)	(6)	(7)	R^2	
ESC1	8	68.712 (1.105)		−35.179 (−0.258)	−147.550 (−0.752)	−6562.000 (−1.107)	149.170 (0.848)	−7.388 (−0.014)	0.660	0.777
ESC2	10	−13.297 (−0.488)		53.081 (1.101)	−24.928 (−0.199)	2832.300 (0.711)	6.334 (0.118)	9.754 (0.049)	0.347	0.462
ESC3	17	−1.932 (−0.128)		−76.858 (−1.586)	−14.635 (−0.177)	541.600 (0.187)	−41.212 (−0.841)	344.840[b] (2.083)	0.336	1.113
ESC4	12	42.894[b] (2.407)	104.230 (0.698)	4.652 (0.091)	41.296 (0.602)	−8817.800 (−1.753)	16.353 (0.331)	−133.270 (−0.563)	0.699	1.943
ESC5	10	24.813 (1.108)		70.800 (0.927)	−120.560 (−0.372)	−3000.700 (−0.672)	−35.712 (−0.502)	−160.180 (−0.526)	0.540	0.942
ESC6	14	12.301 (0.879)		8.541 (0.130)	26.904 (0.145)	2732.000 (0.750)	42.781 (0.988)	−92.397 (−0.479)	0.334	0.801
ESC7	47	−1.593 (−0.266)		4.349 (0.167)	43.161 (0.600)	3385.700[b] (2.462)	7.757 (0.423)	36.672 (0.454)	0.207	2.142
ESC8	43	4.031 (0.705)	−65.748[a] (−1.796)	13.321 (0.499)	23.997 (0.246)	2711.800[a] (1.849)	32.181 (1.324)	28.249 (0.256)	0.372	3.555
ESC9	23	−9.065 (−0.504)	−277.200[c] (−2.756)	−2.735 (−0.069)	−479.700[c] (−2.926)	−944.000 (−0.348)	46.896 (1.349)	500.940[b] (2.270)	0.552	3.294

Retail trade

		(1)	(2)	(3)	(4)	(5)	(6)	(7)	R^2	
ESC1	38	41.696[a] (1.888)	248.720[b] (2.064)	−65.270 (1.306)	0.262[b] (2.133)	8445.100[b] (2.028)	−79.105 (−0.710)	−164.230 (−0.867)	0.355	2.848
ESC2	42	49.977[b] (2.345)	55.318 (0.534)	−24.451 (−0.584)	0.156 (1.273)	−4376.500 (−1.080)	−21.699 (−0.293)	−39.492 (−0.278)	0.194	1.408
ESC3	30	29.275[c] (2.745)	88.780 (0.961)	7.396 (0.220)	−6.223 (−0.201)	3610.900 (0.967)	−14.608 (−0.407)	−124.000 (−1.022)	0.436	2.965
ESC5	15	−3.774 (−0.196)	143.470 (1.645)	50.063 (1.424)	1.264 (0.687)	6667.100 (1.098)	34.554 (0.549)	−1349.610 (−1.663)	0.616	2.141

Table A6-2—Continued

Industry	Number of Observations	RATIO	STD.HRS	WAGE	NEWSEN	ABSEN	UNION	Constant	R^2	F
ESC5	8	-30.451 (-0.603)	373.230 (1.530)	376.050 (1.715)	-95.508 (-1.535)	-1490.200 (-1.589)	-397.860 (-1.311)	-379.990 (-1.035)	0.889	1.344
ESC6	11	34.269 (0.538)	30.203 (0.364)	-32.675 (-0.294)	-7.394 (-0.078)	-1721.600 (-0.253)	-27.100 (-0.342)	8.495 (0.077)	0.210	0.178
ESC7	10	28.569 (0.716)		-38.821 (-0.350)	106.200 (0.845)	438.870 (0.066)	20.584 (0.176)	-25.081 (-0.856)	0.254	0.272
ESC8-9	18	-9.236 (-1.244)	-41.765[b] (-2.340)	-18.579 (-0.857)	-1.296 (-0.950)	3397.60[b] (2.064)	12.209 (0.740)	115.220[b] (2.133)	0.517	1.968
Wholesale trade										
ESC1	72	30.285[b] (2.048)	59.953 (0.531)	-68.010[b] (-2.042)	0.031 (0.350)	-1622.800 (-0.624)	-75.126 (-1.248)	158.960 (1.110)	0.163	2.103
ESC2	75	48.577 (4.593)	42.557 (0.297)	-150.830[c] (-3.900)	-6.496 (-0.912)	-5128.400 (-1.453)	40.946 (0.623)	291.310 (1.695)	0.385	7.105
ESC3	29	1.733 (0.067)		-113.700[a] (-1.947)	-17.317 (-1.348)	-6526.300 (-0.960)	21.137 (0.269)	500.640[c] (2.869)	0.184	1.035
ESC4	34	14.575 (0.971)	-106.210 (-0.699)	-59.697 (-1.445)	-0.182 (-1.537)	30.048 (0.009)	57.965 (1.039)	335.580[a] (1.789)	0.252	1.519
ESC5	12	55.697[a] (1.971)		-90.745 (-1.016)	-6.503 (-0.527)	3918.100 (0.982)	-117.630 (-0.689)	142.180 (0.705)	0.542	1.420
ESC6	12	82.402[b] (2.078)	129.650 (1.079)	58.304 (0.504)	-12.046 (-0.218)	-1712.000 (-1.807)	-107.760 (-0.667)	-369.750 (-0.926)	0.780	2.962
ESC7-9	10	-4.296 (-0.024)		-61.751 (-0.177)	-100.740 (-0.067)	-9500.200 (-0.297)	62.317 (0.288)	429.550 (0.254)	0.332	0.398

[a] Coefficient statistically significantly different from zero at the 0.90 level of significance; two-tailed test.
[b] Coefficient statistically significantly different from zero at the 0.95 level of significance; two-tailed test.
[c] Coefficient statistically significantly different from zero at the 0.99 level of significance; two-tailed test.
Note: Establishment Size Code (ESC): (1) 1–25, (2) 25–50, (3) 50–100, (4) 100–250, (5) 250–500, (6) 500–1000, (7) 1000–2500, (8) and (9) greater than 2500.

Table A6–3. Ratio Coefficient Varies with Establishment Size Class (*t* statistics in parentheses)

$$OT = a_0 + \sum_{j=1}^{9} \alpha_j D_j\, RATIO + a_2\, STD.HRS + a_3\, WAGE + a_4\, NEWSEN + a_5\, ABSEN + a_6\, UNION$$

Industry	Number of Observations	STD.HRS.	WAGE	NEWSEN	ABSEN	UNION	Constant	R^2	F
Construction	285	.990 (0.027)	−28.452[b] (−2.516)	0.007 (0.376)	−1822.300 (−0.321)	−26.081 (−1.023)	139.310[b] (2.535)	0.175	4.430
Transportation	239	175.660 (1.187)	−33.279[a] (−1.660)	0.097[a] (1.883)	630.850 (0.206)	4.594 (0.126)	−147.990 (−0.850)	0.223	4.583
Utilities	184	−55.236 (−1.637)	−6.450 (−0.500)	−15.300 (−0.534)	50.040 (0.061)	17.470 (1.375)	109.670 (1.659)	0.140	1.959
Wholesale Trade	244	63.875 (1.059)	−92.631[c] (−4.967)	−0.028 (−0.404)	−2527.100[a] (−1.751)	4.235 (0.140)	190.270 (2.582)	0.246	5.802
Retail Trade	172	53.195 (1.582)	−18.101 (−1.036)	0.152[b] (2.572)	1152.700 (0.691)	−20.265 (−0.768)	−30.100 (−0.572)	0.226	3.277
Services	89	−27.994 (−0.764)	10.870 (0.712)	−0.021 (−0.442)	−1178.100 (−0.638)	−15.128 (−0.539)	−32.666 (−0.709)	0.306	2.534

[a] Coefficient statistically significantly different from zero at the 0.90 level of significance; two-tailed test.
[b] Coefficient statistically significantly different from zero at the 0.95 level of significance; two-tailed test.
[c] Coefficient statistically significantly different from zero at the 0.99 level of significance; two-tailed test.

Table A6–4. Union–Nonunion Comparisons (*t* statistics in parentheses)

$$OT = a_0 + a_1\,RATIO + a_2\,STD.HRS + a_3\,WAGE + a_4\,NEWSEN + a_5\,ABSEN$$

Industry Group	Number of Observations	RATIO	STD.HRS	WAGE	NEWSEN	ABSEN	Constant	R^2	F
Mining									
(A)	37	-2.205 (-0.287)	1.494 (0.013)	-47.611[b] (-2.015)	0.097[a] (1.727)	-4552.800[b] (-2.094)	328.980[b] (2.669)	0.452	5.118
(N)	17	11.994 (0.596)	13.987 (0.085)	-15.266 (-0.277)	0.085 (0.920)	-1330.00 (-1.301)	203.410 (0.966)	0.365	1.266
(U)	20	-7.196 (-1.037)		-112.780 (-0.331)	0.024 (0.244)	-2841.700[a] (-1.938)	214.970[a] (1.931)	0.366	2.171
Construction									
(A)	284	30.276[b] (5.913)	6.943 (0.191)	-29.351[c] (-3.080)	0.004 (0.217)	-3064.900 (-0.536)	119.890[b] (2.217)	0.126	8.050
(N)	100	30.879 (2.894)	30.723 (0.600)	-23.102 (-1.339)	0.027 (0.784)	-1903.40 (-0.287)	63.672 (0.678)	0.122	2.653
(U)	184	31.119[c] (5.100)	-11.775 (-0.263)	-28.102[a] (-1.789)	-0.010 (-0.398)	-1039.200 (-0.796)	137.360 (1.653)	0.136	5.612
Transportation									
(A)	239	40.572[c] (5.803)	130.030 (0.806)	-43.182[b] (-2.463)	0.102[a] (1.934)	-880.650 (-0.297)	-51.385 (-0.294)	0.137	7.440
(N)	53	48.042[b] (2.607)		-84.512[a] (-1.897)	0.102 (1.282)	-1637.900 (-0.295)	153.940 (1.193)	0.171	2.488
(U)	186	43.705[c] (4.804)	127.100 (0.857)	-12.155 (-0.511)	0.090 (0.831)	-1371.800 (-0.349)	-167.080 (-0.919)	0.132	5.493
Utilities									
(A)	184	8.214[b] (2.143)	-64.391[a] (-1.949)	-7.942 (-0.645)	3.431 (0.124)	456.810 (0.590)	141.160[b] (2.211)	0.077	2.968
(N)	58	10.878 (1.425)	-19.081 (-0.184)	-20.219 (-0.818)	31.845 (0.658)	73.433 (0.041)	107.150 (0.705)	0.063	0.700
(U)	126	3.574 (0.769)	-95.425[b] (-2.691)	6.499 (0.411)	-31.707 (0.902)	327.020 (0.382)	170.580[b] (2.218)	0.117	3.173

Table A6–4—*Continued*

	N							R^2	F
Wholesale trade									
(A)	244	38.980^c (6.544)	49.306 (0.833)	−103.130^c (−6.195)	−0.031 (−2.187)	−3130.200^b (−2.187)	207.300^c (2.997)	0.240	15.050
(N)	147	44.350^c (5.518)	51.358 (0.668)	−125.020^c (−5.064)	−0.013 (−0.149)	−3804.300^a (−1.742)	230.050^b (2.465)	0.287	11.389
(U)	97	25.331 (2.781)	−7.634 (−0.080)	−54.806^b (−2.024)	−0.081 (−0.715)	−2687.800 (−1.586)	205.750^a (1.712)	0.132	2.760
Retail trade									
(A)	172	32.582^c (4.429)	57.772^a (1.920)	−1.968 (−1.212)	0.168^c (2.856)	1013.400 (0.619)	−37.439 (−0.779)	0.163	6.492
(N)	116	34.475^c (3.562)	81.417^b (1.983)	−17.062 (0.706)	0.203^c (2.836)	1383.000 (0.617)	−62.090 (−0.943)	0.197	5.416
(U)	56	32.193^c (2.921)	−1.938 (−0.049)	18.972 (0.849)	−0.015 (−0.130)	−4190.100 (−0.690)	−84.557 (−1.147)	0.163	1.948
Services									
(A)	89	36.086^c (4.203)	−33.568 (−0.928)	10.701 (0.722)	−0.014 (−0.284)	−4106.800 (−0.977)	−36.482 (−0.807)	0.223	4.764
(N)	57	45.324^c (3.779)	−24.291 (−0.535)	11.964 (0.431)	−0.0008 (−0.012)	−2859.500 (−1.393)	−61.141 (−0.975)	0.257	3.524
(U)	32	31.161^b (2.199)	−80.340 (−1.143)	16.000 (1.032)	−0.035 (−0.393)	818.390 (0.306)	−7.679 (−0.105)	0.253	1.766

[a] Coefficient statistically significantly different from zero at the 0.90 level of significance; two-tailed test.
[b] Coefficient statistically significantly different from zero at the 0.95 level of significance; two-tailed test.
[c] Coefficient statistically significantly different from zero at the 0.99 level of significance; two-tailed test.
(A) All establishments, (N) nonunionized only, (U) unionized only.

Table A6-5. Data Segmented by Component Two-Digit Industries

$$OT = a_0 + a_1 RATIO + a_2 STD.HRS + a_3 WAGE + a_4 NEWSEN + a_5 ABSEN + a_6 UNION$$

S.I.C. Code	Number of Observations	RATIO	STD.HRS	WAGE	NEWSEN	ABSEN	UNION	Constant	R^2	F
Construction										
15	210	31.793^c (6.792)	12.433 (1.348)	-11.495 (-1.032)	0.005 (0.273)	-3683.400 (-0.576)	-35.050 (-1.501)	52.728 (0.969)	0.195	5.207
16	26	33.433 (0.976)	176.760 (0.830)	-80.842 (-1.664)	-0.074 (-0.670)	-1978.500 (-1.316)	111.060 (0.882)	167.680^a (0.580)	0.212	0.852
17	49	15.906 (0.661)	29.778 (0.254)	-30.100 (-.729)	0.074 (1.034)	767.194 (0.020)	8.013 (0.836)	147.710 (0.811)	0.041	0.300
Transportation										
40	43	11.475 (0.469)	41.343 (0.540)	-85.005 (-1.227)	-76.395 (-0.696)	3362.700 (0.636)	-19.494 (-0.111)	283.500 (0.907)	0.109	0.736
42	196	49.374^c (5.719)		-46.188^b (-2.118)	0.112^b (2.026)	883.850 (0.264)	178.080 (0.453)	53.436^a (0.746)	0.192	9.000
Utilities										
48	19	26.987 (1.120)	-10.938 (-0.074)	-10.558 (-0.124)	-129.200 (-1.222)	2374.000 (0.618)	13.047 (0.062)	-53.197 (-0.110)	0.594	2.923
49	165	5.607 (1.363)	-22.848 (-0.319)	-2.988^b (-2.153)	11.656 (0.398)	97.222 (0.120)	9.652 (0.737)	102.510 (1.194)	0.020	0.545

Table A6–5—*Continued*

Retail trade									
52	20	7.594 (0.438)		−181.830[b] (−2.095)	0.112 (0.981)	4118.200 (1.042)	159.820 (0.929)	506.780[b] (2.609)	0.441	2.211
53	35	4.398 (0.432)	20.822 (1.009)	−21.736 (−0.811)	−0.271 (−0.249)	−696.400 (−0.373)	15.722 (0.660)	62.250 (1.192)	0.093	0.497
54	41	12.357 (0.994)	43.949 (0.837)	56.407 (1.908)	−0.001 (−0.012)	−1724.700 (−0.800)	−23.835 (−0.703)	−89.536 (−1.135)	0.179	1.235
55	26	88.445[c] (3.581)	60.106 (0.439)	−48.804 (−1.164)	7.891 (0.431)	−4229.500 (−0.799)	2.221 (0.031)	−124.840 (−0.701)	0.537	3.678
56, 57	15	−14.320 (−0.841)	35.788 (0.563)	−28.591 (−1.095)	−27.906 (−1.184)	−813.070 (−0.272)	37.036 (0.808)	184.740 (1.529)	0.225	0.387
58	21	14.769 (1.291)	−34.368 (−0.902)	22.631 (0.940)	−0.038 (−0.685)	−3423.400 (−0.983)	−34.815 (−1.175)	10.093 (0.143)	0.268	0.854
59	14	110.940 (1.449)	60.438 (0.087)	6.301 (0.022)	0.726 (1.564)	−1839.500 (−0.097)	−123.500 (−0.459)	−373.230 (0.307)	0.400	0.779

[a] Coefficient statistically significantly different from zero at the 0.90 level of significance; two-tailed test.
[b] Coefficient statistically significantly different from zero at the 0.95 level of significance; two-tailed test.
[c] Coefficient statistically significantly different from zero at the 0.99 level of significance; two-tailed test.

Bibliography

[1] Aigner, D., and Chu, S. "On Estimating the Industry Production Function," *American Economic Review* 58 (September 1968).

[2] Arrow, K. *Applications of Control Theory to Economic Growth.* Technical Report No. 2. Institute for Mathematical Studies in the Social Sciences, Stanford University, July 1967.

[3] Ashar, V., and Wallace, T., "A Sampling Study of Minimum Absolute Deviations Estimators." *Operations Research* 11 (1963).

[4] Ball, J., and St. Cyr, E. "Short-Term Employment Functions in British Manufacturing Industries." *Review of Economic Studies* 33 (July 1966).

[5] Barzel, Y. "The Determinants of Daily Hours and Wages." Unpublished manuscript, October 1969.

[6] Becker, G. *Human Capital: A Theoretical and Empirical Analysis with Special Reference to Education.* New York: National Bureau of Economic Research 1964.

[7] Becker, J. *Guaranteed Income for the Unemployed: The Story of S.U.B.* Baltimore, Johns Hopkins Press, 1968.

[8] Black, S., and Kelejian, H. "A Macro Model of the U.S. Labor Market." Princeton University Working Paper No. 10. September 1968.

[9] Brechling, F. P., "The Relationship Between Output and Employment in *British Manufacturing Industries.*" *Review of Economic Studies* 32 (July 1965).

[10] ———, and O'Brien, P. "Short-Run Employment Functions in Manufacturing Industries: An International Comparison." *Review of Economics and Statistics* 49 (August 1967).

[11] Bronfenbrenner, M., and Mossin, J. "The Shorter Work Week and the Labor Supply." *Southern Economic Journal* 33 (January 1967).

[12] Bry, G. *The Average Workweek as an Economic Indicator.* Occasional Paper No. 69. New York: National Bureau of Economic Research, 1959.

[13] Chamber of Commerce of the United States, *Fringe Benefits*, various issues 1947–1965.

[14] Chapman, S. "Hours of Labor." *Economic Journal* 17 (September 1909).

[15] Charnes, A.; Cooper, W.; and Ferguson, R. "Optimal Estimation of Executive Compensation by Linear Programming," *Management Science*, 2, 1955.

[16] Chow, G. "Tests of Equality Between Sets of Coefficients in Two Linear Regressions." *Econometrica*, 28 (July 1960).

[17] Coen, R., and Hickman, B. "Aggregative Demand Functions for Capital and Labor in the U.S. Economy." Stanford University Research Memoranda No. 74, July 1969.

[18] Cook, A. "A Generalized CES Production Function: An Analysis of Labor Employment in Manufacturing Industries." Presented to the Econometric Society Meetings, December 1968.

[19] Cotterill, P. "A Model of Labor in Retail Trade," Ph.D. dissertation, Northwestern University, June 1969.

[20] Douglas, P. *Theory of Wages.* New York: 1934.

[21] Dymond, W., and Saunders, G. "Hours of Work in Canada." In *Hours of Work*, edited by C. Danhert, Evanston: Harper and Row, 1966.

[22] Fair, R. *The Short-Run Demand for Workers and Hours.* Contributions to Economic Analysis, vol. 59. Amsterdam: North-Holland, 1969.

[23] Feldstein, M. "Specification of the Labor Input in the Aggregate Production Function." *Review of Economic Studies* 34 (October 1968).

[24] ———. "Estimating the Supply Curve of Working Hours." *Oxford Economic Papers* 20 (August 1968).

[25] ———. "A Theory of Labor Supply." Unpublished manuscript, 1966.

[26] Finegan, T. "Hours of Work in the United States: A Cross-Section Analysis." *Journal of Political Economy* 70 (December 1962).

[27] Fisher, W. "A Note on Curve Fitting with Minimum Deviations by Linear Programming." *Journal of the American Statistical Association* 56 (1961).

[28] Fuchs, V. *The Service Economy.* General Series No. 87. New York: National Bureau of Economic Research, 1968.

[29] Garbarino, J. "Fringe Benefits and Overtime as Barriers to Expanding Employment." *Industrial and Labor Relations Review* 17 (April 1964).

[30] Gelfand, I., and Fomin, S. *Calculus of Variations*, Englewood Cliffs, N.J.: Prentice-Hall, 1963.

[31] Hamermesh, D. "A Disaggregative Econometric Model of Gross Changes in Employment." Cowles Foundation Discussion Paper, October 1968.

[32] Hardy, G.; Littlewood, J.; and Polya, G. *Inequalities.* New York: Cambridge University Press, 1934.

[33] Hildebrand, G., and Delehanty, G. "Wage Levels and Differentials." In *Prosperity and Unemployment*, edited by R. Gordon and M. Gordon. New York: Wiley, 1966.

[34] Hoel, P. *Introduction to Mathematical Statistics.* (3rd ed.) New York: Wiley, 1962.

[35] Holt, C.; Modigliani, F.; Muth, J. and Simon, H. *Planning Production, Inventories and Work Force.* Englewood Cliffs, N.J.: Prentice-Hall, 1961.

[36] Hughes, B. "The Automobile Industry Compensation Structure." Draft of a chapter of an unfinished Ph.D. dissertation, Princeton University, received from Professor A. Rees in October 1968.

[37] Johnston, J. *Econometric Methods*. New York: McGraw-Hill, 1963.

[38] Kerr, C. "The Balkanization of Labor Markets." In *Labor Mobility and Economic Opportunity*, edited by E. Bakke. Cambridge: M.I.T. Press, 1954.

[39] Ketchum, E. "The Demand for Man-Hours in Manufacturing Industries." Unpublished research paper, Princeton University, April 1968.

[40] Kosters, M. *Income and Substiiution Effects in a Family Labor Supply Model*. Santa Monica: Rand Corporation, 1966.

[41] Kuh, E. "Income Distribution and Employment Over the Business Cycle." In *The Brookings Quarterly Econometric Model of the United States*, Chicago: edited by J. Duesenberry, G. Fromm, and E. Kuh. Rand McNally, 1965.

[42] ———. "Cyclical and Secular Labor Productivity in U.S. Manufacturing." *Review of Economics and Statistics* 47 (February 1965).

[43] Lewis, H. "Hours of Work and Hours of Leisure." *Industrial Relations Research Association Proceedings* 9, 1957.

[44] Lucas, R., and Rapping, L. "Real Wages, Employment and Inflation." *Journal of Political Economy* 77 (October 1969).

[45] Macdonald, R. "The Fringe Barrier Hypothesis and Overtime Behavior: Comment." *Industrial and Labor Relations Review* 19 (July 1966).

[46] Malinvaud, E. *Statistical Methods in Econometrics*. Chicago: Rand McNally, 1966.

[47] Mortensen, D. T. "Short Run Employment and Production Decisions." Mimeographed. Northwestern University, September 1969.

[48] Moses, L. "Income, Leisure, and Wage Pressure." *Economic Journal* 72 (June 1962).

[49] Murphy, G. *Ordinary Differential Equations and Their Solutions*. New York: Van Nostrand, 1960.

[50] Nadiri, M. I. "The Effects of Relative Prices and Capacity on the Demand for Labor in U.S. Manufacturing." *Review of Economic Studies* 34 (July 1968).

[51] Nadiri, M. I., and Rosen, S. "Interrelated Factor Demand." *American Economic Review* 59 (September 1969).

[52] Oi, W. "Labor as a Quasi-Fixed Factor." *Journal of Political Economy* 70 (1962).

[53] Orrbeck, M.; Schutte, D.; and Thompson, H. "The Effect of Worker Productivity on Production Smoothing." *Management Science* (Series B), February 1968.

[54] Perlman, R. "Observations on Overtime and Moonlighting." *Southern Economic Journal* 32 (October 1966).

[55] ———. *Labor Theory*. New York: Wiley, 1969.

[56] Pontryagin, L. S.; Boltyanskii, V. G.; Gamkrelidze, R. V.; and Mishehenko, E. F. *The Mathematical Theory of Optimal Processes.* New York: Wiley, 1962.

[57] Reder, M. "Theory of Occupational Wage Differentials," *American Economic Review* 45 (1955).

[58] Rosen, S. "Short-Run Employment Variations on Class-I Railroads in the U.S. 1947–63." *Econometrica* 37 (December 1968).

[59] ———. "On the Interindustry Wage and Hours Structure." *Journal of Political Economy* 77 (February 1969).

[60] Rothschild, M., "Changing Demand: Its Costs and Consequences." Paper presented to the Econometric Society Meetings, December 1968.

[61] Rothschild, M., and Stiglitz, J. "Increasing Risk: A Definition and Its Economic Consequences." Discussion Paper No. 275. New Haven Cowles Foundation, 1969.

[62] Scheffe, H. *The Analysis of Variance.* New York: Wiley, 1959.

[63] Smith, K. "The Effect of Uncertainty on Monopoly Price, Capital Stock and Utilization of Capital." *Journal of Economic Theory* 1 (June 1969).

[64] ———. "Risk and Optimal Utilization of Capital." *Review of Economic Studies* 37 (April 1970).

[65] Smyth, D., and Ireland, N. "Short-Term Employment Functions in Australian Manufacturing." *Review of Economics and Statistics* 49 (November 1967).

[66] Soligo, R. "Short-Run Relationship Between Employment and Output." *Yale Economic Essays* (Spring 1966).

[67] Solow, R. "Short-Run Adjustment of Employment to Output." In *Value Capital and Growth*, edited by N. Wolfe. New York: Oxford University Press, 1968.

[68] Theil, H. *Lecture Notes on Econometrics.* Unpublished manuscript. (Chapter 11 on Specification Analysis.)

[69] Treadway, A. "Rational Entrepreneurial Behavior and the Dynamics of Investment." Ph.D. dissertation, University of Chicago, 1967.

[70] U.S. Congress. *Overtime Pay Penalty Act of 1964.* Hearing Before the Subcommittee on Labor, House of Representatives, 88th Congress, 2nd Session on H. R. 1680 and H.R. 9802 (3 volumes).

[71] U.S. Department of Labor. *Premium Pay for Overtime under the Fair Labor Standards Act November 1967* (submitted to Congress 1968).

[72] ———. *Statistics on Manpower*, March 1969.

[73] ———. *Retail Trade: A Study to Measure the Effects of the Minimum Wage and Maximum Hours Standards of the Fair Labor Standards Act* (submitted to Congress, January 1967).

[74] ———. Bureau of Employment Security, *Unemployment Insurance: State Laws and Experience*, Bulletin U-198R, 1965.

[75] ———, ———. *Unemployment Insurance Tax Rates by Industry, 1964, Bulletin* U-255, 1965.

[76] U.S. Department of Labor, Bureau of Employment Security. *State Workmens Compensation Laws*, Bulletin 161, 1964.

[77] ———, Bureau of Labor Statistics. *Employment and Earning Statistics for the United States, 1909–1967*, Bulletin 1312–5, 1967.

[78] ———, ———. *Employer Expenditures for Selected Remuneration Practices for Production Workers in Manufacturing Industries, 1959*, Bulletin 1308, January 1962.

[79] ———, ———. *Employer Expenditures for Selected Supplementary Compensation Practices for Production and Related Workers' Manufacturing Industries*, 1962, Bulletin 1428, April 1965.

[80] ———, ———. *Employee Compensation in the Private Nonfarm Economy, 1966*, Bulletin 1627, June 1969.

[81] ———, ———. *Wage Chronologies* (various issues).

[82] ———, ———. *Digest of 100 Selected Health and Insurance Plans Under Collective Bargaining Early 1966*, Bulletin 1502, 1967.

[83] ———, ———. *Financing Supplementary Unemployment Benefit Plans 1966*, Bulletin 1483, 1967.

[84] ———, ———. *Premium Pay Provisions for Weekend Work in Seven Continuous Process Industries 1966*, Bulletin 1480, 1966.

[85] ———, ———. *Major Collective Bargaining Agreements: Severance Pay and Layoff Benefit Plans*, Bulletin 1425_2, 1965.

[86] ———, ———. *Major Collective Bargaining Agreements: S.U.B. Plans and Wage-Employment Guarantees*, Bulletin 1425–3, 1965.

[87] ———, *Wage, Hours, and Public Contracts Division. Fair Labor Standards Act of 1938, as Amended*, November 1966.

[88] Van Atta, S. "An Analysis of Overtime Hours for Production Workers in Manufacturing Industries, 1957–65." Ph.D. dissertation, University of California at Berkeley, December 1967.

[89] Wagner, H. "Linear Programming Techniques for Regression Analysis." *Journal of the American Statistical Association* 54 (1959).

[90] Waud, R. "Manhour Behavior in U.S. Manufacturing: A Neoclassical Interpretation." *Journal of Political Economy* 76 (February 1968).

[91] Zellner, A. "Linear Regressions with Inequality Constraints on the Coefficients." Mimeographed report no. 6109. Louvain International Center for Management Science, 1961.